PRAISE FOR FIGHTS LIKE A GIRL

"When I enlisted in the Air Force in 1976 at 17 years old, I wasn't told that serving in the military as a female was an anomaly. What I was told by my recruiter is that I would receive travel, training, and an education. The Air Force lived up to its promise. If that means I was trained to *Fight Like A Girl*, because I am one, then I did do to the best of my ability right alongside the best AIR "MEN" ever. I am so grateful to Pete Mecca for finding merit in sharing these stories of strength and determination."

— **Patricia S. Blassie, Colonel, USAF retired**

Fights Like A Girl

Todo,
Thank you for your support and
for what you do. Enjoy the stories!
Pete Mecca

Fights Like A Girl

WOMEN WARRIORS: PAST TO PRESENT

PETE MECCA

" WHOEVER SAID THE PEN IS MIGHTIER THAN
THE SWORD OBVIOUSLY NEVER ENCOUNTERED
AUTOMATIC WEAPONS! "

- DOUGLAS MACARTHUR -

Deeds Publishing | Athens

Published by Deeds Publishing in Athens, GA
www.deedspublishing.com

Printed in The United States of America

Cover design by Mark Babcock.

ISBN 978-1-950794-34-8

Books are available in quantity for promotional or premium use. For information, email info@deedspublishing.com.

First Edition, 2021

10 9 8 7 6 5 4 3 2 1

For my beautiful wife, Joyce.
See you in heaven, Baby.

*L to R — Frances Green, Margaret Kirchner, Ann Waldner, and
Blanche Osborn leave their B-17 Pistol Packin' Mama*

Contents

'Her voice was crystal clear and rang like a temple bell. She stood nine feet tall and her breasts were three feet long.'

Preface

Ever since mankind was kicked out of the Garden of Eden or clambered down from the treetops — take your pick — then started squabbling over munchies and mates, which brought about the nasty habit of hurling stones at one another, womankind has been omnipresent flinging the identical rocks with deadly precision. He *'fights like a girl'* has long been an insult of sorts to describe a male deprived of brawling talents, a sissy or a wussy, who relies on biting ears or scratching out those proverbial eyeballs. Nevertheless, in wars and disputes throughout warmongering history, the fairer sex has *fought like, and many times, fought better,* than their male counterparts. In countless battles, women warriors commanded the male genera in combat.

Lady warriors of yesteryear habitually paid a heavy price for trespassing on male turf given that *'civilization'* has been predominantly governed by the male species. Joan of Arc is the customary exemplar. Late in the Hundred Years' War against England, she lifted the siege of Orleans in only nine days and by the age of 17 performed an important role in the French army. Frenchmen loyal to England, known as the Burgundians, captured Joan in 1430, tried and convicted the teenage generalissimo of heresy then burned her to death bound to a stake at the age of 19. A 19 year old teenager, a God-fearing youngster, led French soldiers into combat and helped save her country, yet was admonished by a male-dominated Burgundian turncoat court. Joan's guilty verdict was overturned by the Pope 24 years later, posthumously. The world would wait another 460 years before she was canonized a saint by Pope Benedict XV in 1920.

The slaughter of humans in a male dominated world does not bode well for men, yet women can be and have been as savage, uncompromising, strategic, and courageous as their male counterparts. In contemporary society, the softer of our species has proven to be gifted enough to join the ranks of men in the majority of MOS (military occupation specialty) positions. The military doors of opportunity have been flung wide open for women and they are more than proving their worthiness.

My genesis for *Fights Like a Girl* found fertile writing-ground while peddling my first paperback, *Veterans: Stories From America's Best*, during a literary festival in Milton, Georgia, an event held on a Saturday and Sunday after three days of torrential downpours which dissipated that weekend into a penetrating mist. The waterlogged ground sloshed mud around one's go-to-Sunday shoes, or tennis shoes, which absorbed the H2O like a sponge. I say that with sincere honesty since yours truly was one of the numerous tennis shoe-wearing victims.

Dozens of Hemingway Wannabes braved the elements to participate in hour long question and answer meet-the-writer sessions under the shelter of canvas event tents (you know the type, square with plastic fake windows) with a so-called floor of black muddy gook. To add to our discomfort, it was bone-jarring cold inside the canvas. Outside gadgets mistakenly identified as portable heaters blew lukewarm baby-breaths into each igloo (tent) through a cannibalized rubber gutter downspout peeking under the canvas. The heating contraptions generated enough warmth to possibly keep the guest-author nearest the downspout from teeth-chattering too noisily. I grabbed the cold metal folding chair closest to the lukewarm baby-breaths, another male author glued himself to the frozen chair next to mine, and the lady author (I refrained from using the word 'authoress' since the expression is now considered old-fashioned and sexist…but I digress), sat furthest from the inadequate heat on a wobbly makeshift stage. Gentlemen, we weren't.

There were enough folding chairs inside the tent for about 50 folks. I counted six attendees, all sitting in a covey near the downspout. After an hour-long cold-weather endurance test, yours truly and the other two authors made a dash for the book store for book signings and central heating. Other writers had beaten us to the warmest spots, but any spot in the book store was warmer than the event tents. Nonetheless, warmed and refreshed via pricey bottled water, roughly a dozen novelists, poets, even one playwright, stood or sat behind rectangular folding tables to hopefully sell and sign their literary handiwork.

I noticed three ladies peddling and signing books as if three young'uns were hawking mud-pies (sorry, I couldn't help but reference mud again) to naïve neighborhood buddies. And they were selling a LOT of those mud-pies. Inquisitive me started asking questions and discovered the ladies had written their book as a trio and were on the New York Times best-seller list. And their New York Times best-seller was selling out. The book shop owner hurried into a storage room, returned with more copies of their handiwork, and the trio kept on signing and selling. What, pray tell, had this female trio written?

As our hour long signing event concluded and other frozen authors came in to enjoy their hour of warmth, the three ladies (Beatriz Williams, Lauren Willig, and Karen White) stopped by my table for a short tête-à-tête as I was counting the huge amount of money I made from selling four books. I ascertained their New York Times' best-seller "*The Glass Ocean*" relayed the loves and lives of three amazing women (one in recent times, two in the past) linked to the tragic sinking in international waters of the British luxury liner, *Lusitania*, by a German submarine on May 7, 1915.

They showed interest in my paperback on veterans and asked if any women were represented within its pages. "Of course," I said. "I have interviewed around forty female veterans." Beatriz suggested, "Then interview more, and write another book on noteworthy female warriors from days gone by with your present-day interviewees bringing up the rear. Listen, in this day and age books on women and blacks sell, period. Have a nice day, and good luck to you." With that, the trio promenaded out of the book store.

I stood in stunned silence, having been pointed to the yellow brick road for frustrated authors. *Sounds doable*, I thought, then completed my sales count. A lucrative payday: enough money to purchase gas and buy two Krystal cheeseburgers. Yet, the idea of a book on lady warriors gradually energized the creative portion on the right side of my brain then penetrated the dead cells of writing ability on the left side of my noggin. In layman's terms, I had a hell of a headache. Even so, somewhere in that blob of gray matter a spark of creativity sallied forth.

So, here we go: The Book, written by a male on the advice of three females. There should be a clever little anecdote attached to that last sentence, but I can't think of one.

I write with humor. That's who I am. History is boring to a lot of folks, especially young folks, so my humorist tendency scribbling libretti has only two purposes:

1. To grab and drag the uninterested into the fascinating world of history, a topic destined to repeat its shoddier events if not studied and retained. The examination of history, as I was taught while struggling through middle school and high school back in the days of Tyrannosaurus X, was principally the task of remembering names and dates, as in boring! Many of my classmates faded away from history and entered the

creepy world of calculus, a subject I wouldn't touch with a ten foot pole, much less a #2 pencil. Anyway, in my humble opinion, history taught with insightful wittiness would be the catalysis for a rebirth of interest in a subject routinely avoided by a majority of young scholars. Make history enjoyable. Admittedly, history text is clogged with death, despots, destruction, deities, and disasters, but such is the reality of life, the good, the bad, and the ugly.

2. To grab and drag yours truly away from the serious side of penning war stories. I saw and smelled and heard and felt the ugliness of war in Vietnam for 30 months, an ugliness I care not to revisit unless absolutely necessary. Amid the ugliness, however, the Phoenix of humor would somehow arise to dampen the dreadfulness of death and destruction. A good laugh in Vietnam was the mental medic of that war. Bull shit bred sanity.

Prepare yourself to learn about a few ladies you may not want to offend. No bull shit.

The Book: A few lady warriors of long ago will be given credit as a precursor to the interviews I've conducted with female veterans in my several years of writing veteran's stories. Ladies have long held down the home front, and I consider these women as veterans in their own right. The six branches of military service, the Army, Navy, Air Force, Marines, Coast Guard, and the newly established Space Force, have two rarely mentioned and overlooked siblings: the Home Front and the Merchant Marines. The Merchant Marines had the second highest casualty rate percentage-wise during WWII than all the other service branches, with the United State Marine Corps as the exception. The historical neglect of our Merchant Marines is shameful.

However, this tome is about women warriors, the fairer sex, who were unfair, unashamed, unafraid, and unapologetic to take up arms, slice and dice arms with weapons, and kill before being killed. Ladies who sought revenge for rape or torture or both, and exhibited no mercy in combat. In spite of this, female warriors often show signs of compassion as befitting a motherly image.

The internet and libraries (buildings brimming with books, remember? But I digress, once again) tender a plethora of information on women in war. Visit a library; expand your knowledge. Albeit, my intention as previously mentioned is to point out a few lady warriors from yester-year before giving a voice to the female warriors of today. As I advise all veterans, 'If you made it out of boot camp, you have a story to tell', which is the honest truth. I have over 400 interviews under my brass belt buckle with brothers and sisters from all conflicts, all services and ranks. Therefore, I proudly dedicate the following narratives to the ladies who wore armor and the ladies who serve in armored divisions today. They, who bear our children, are also prepared to bear arms against those who would slay our children.

The English playwright and poet, William Congreve, wrote in Act 3, Scene 2, of *The Morning Bride*, circa 1697, "Hell hath no fury as a woman scorned." Well, Mr. Congreve, the threat is doubled if she's toting an M-16.

Enhance Your Knowledge

Read. *Read.* READ. *READ.* Especially you ladies. The female warriors mentioned thus far, and many thousands more, were and are your sisters. They led the way. They crushed brick wall barriers and were willing to pay the price; even more amazing, by doing so they earned the respect and loyalty of the men under their commands.

Learn of Artemisia I of Caria, the female naval commander and ally of the King of Persia, Xerxes. Yes, as in the movie, *300: Rise of an Empire.*

Learn of Lozen, the female warrior and prophet of the Chihenne Chiricahua Apache. She rode and fought beside the likes of Victorio and Geronimo.

At least 400 women fought alongside the men during the American Civil War, including Lizzie Hoffman, a black lady from Virginia. She joined the U.S. 45th Colored Infantry and fought for two years disguised as a man until her secret was 'exposed' by her fellow soldiers while boarding a steamer. Lizzie was put under arrest then charged for masquerading as a man. Her penalty: Lizzie was required to wear a dress.

Lt. Annie G. Fox was on duty as chief nurse at Hickam Air Field in Hawaii on December 7, 1941. During the Japanese attack, as bombs exploded and bullets whizzed through the air, Annie worked around-the-clock caring for the wounded and dying. She was the first woman to be awarded a Purple Heart, but with a slight drawback. Annie was never wounded. Not until 1944 did requirements change: battle wounds *only* to qualify a soldier for a Purple Heart. Her medal was rescinded, but Annie did receive the Bronze Star in its place.

Zoya Kosmodemyanskaya was executed by the Germans during WWII for guerilla activities, including sabotage and setting land mines. She was the first women to be awarded the title of 'Hero of the Soviet Union' during the war. Zoya was tortured by German soldiers, stripped, whipped, and marched around naked in the bitter cold. After her hanging, Zoya's body was left dangling on display for over a month. She had just turned 18.

Now it's up to you. Learn and teach the stories of these women, or let them lapse into the bottomless pit of forgotten history. Those are the only two choices available. I've had the honor to interview contemporary lady warriors plus researched and composed the stories of long-gone female combatants for my full-page newspaper column, "A Veteran's Story." So, why on God's green earth am I given a full page in newspapers to tell the tale? Because the public is starving for this knowledge, especially young folks who are no longer taught genuine history but revised interpretations by less-than-accurate agenda-motivated academics. When history is given a face-lift to make the objectionable and unpleasant seem more palatable, Pandora's Box of identical mistakes and suffering will open and reoccur, and not for the good of mankind, nor womankind.

Enjoy the stories.

Stories Via Personal Interviews

A pithy introduction, if I may do so. The reader will quickly discover my writing is seriously lacking intellectual content, mainly because there's not an intellectual bone in my body. But that's a good thing, since my intention is not to impress but to inform. The stories henceforth are unassuming narratives from unpretentious people who, through their experiences with or in the military, war, or rebellion, have extraordinary stories to tell.

The military transforms people, from the ones on the Home Front dealing with separation anxiety to the young recruit standing butt-naked in a room full of other butt-naked recruits being poked and tested and evaluated to see if they're qualified to give their life if necessary for their country. And it is for their country, for as Mark Twain eloquently declared, *"Loyalty to country always, loyalty to government, when it deserves it."*

Is a man or woman willing to face death in combat because they hate what is in front of them, or because they love what they left behind them? Is a call to duty an act of patriotism, or a desire to earn a license to kill? These questions and many more concerning military duty can only be answered by the individual who takes an oath to defend this great country against all enemies, both foreign and domestic. '*Something bigger than yourself*' is a favored catchphrase in answering the question, "*Why?*"

Why? Why does an individual virtually sign away their life to join an organization for low wages and long hours? Why are they motivated to follow the lead of a Commander-in-Chief they may distrust or dislike? A Few Good Men, Aim High, Join the Navy and See the World, An Army of One, or as the Coast Guard candidly cautions, "You have to go out, but you don't have to come back." Why would a rational person put their own life in jeopardy for total strangers?

The following stories answer a few of those questions since every veteran had or has their own motive to sign on the dotted line. They retain their own individual experiences, pain, emotional ailments, success and failure, good or bad health, good or bad teeth, good or bad offspring, for they are human beings, just like you and me, but with one distinct difference: Their membership in an exclusive club open only to those who qualify. And to qualify, all you have to do is sign your life away.

These are the stories of ladies who qualified.

Elizabeth "Bubba" McClain
Major Bubba

Major Bubba retiring in 1962

No, this is not the narrative of a tobacco-chewing six-toothed pick-up-truck-drivin' country bumpkin who qualified for a cameo appearance in the acclaimed action-adventure movie *Deliverance*. There's no catchy banjo music playing in the background or a city-dweller versus redneck analogy since this lady 'Bubba' is genuine, served as a registered nurse in WWII, and wore a skirt. Admittedly, this lovely southern lady, Elizabeth McClain, is the first female I've ever met with the nickname 'Bubba', but bizarre things happen, especially in rural Pelham, Georgia circa 1912.

You would think an individual old enough to remember The Great

War (now referred to as World War One) and bounced along Georgia backroads in a rattle-trap Tin Lizzie during the Roarin' Twenties, plus survived The Great Depression and didn't see a parked airplane until the age of 27, would be a wealth of knowledge concerning her life, her country, and a plethora of changes mother earth experienced leading up to the year 2011 when she granted the first interview ever about her military service during World War Two and the decades of years in between. Yeah, you may think that, but you would be thinking wrong.

Elizabeth "Bubba" McClain is an American icon, a well-mannered, well-bred southern lady of The Greatest Generation who still remembers when ladies acted like, well, ladies. Her niece, Mrs. Louise Melton, contacted me to ask if I'd be interested in interviewing her aunt, a retired WWII veteran and resident of an assisted living facility called Morningside. Mrs. Melton mentioned that her aunt served in WWII as a registered nurse, enlisted in the U.S. Army in 1942 as a 2nd Lieutenant, and retired as a Major in 1962. I pounced on the opportunity. With Mrs. Melton as intermediary, we teamed up to interview a gem of a woman with deep-seated devotion to family and country, and as I soon discovered, a lady of very few words.

As sweet as Southern iced tea with Georgia Peach good manners bred of small town living and good parents, Elizabeth McClain is the matronly lady everyone wants for their grandmother, or in this case, their great-great grandmother. Ambulatory only for short distances, Elizabeth arrived via wheelchair for the interview in the Morningside dining hall. A pleasant face with a pleasant smile, she shook my hand and stated, "Nice to meet you." Those four words 'nice to meet you' was one of the longest sentences she produced during a two hour interview.

As you might expect, Elizabeth's niece, Mrs. Melton filled in areas sorely in need of dialogue. The lack of expression was not from senility or disinterest for the interview, but rather an acceptance of the fact that whatever happens between birth and your last day on this side of the grass is really no big deal. In my opinion, I believe that's a pretty decent philosophy from a Southern Belle who has lived her entire life with 'Bubba' for a nickname. To be truthful, much of Elizabeth's dialog is essentially additional comments by her niece to lengthen short answers like, 'I reckon' or 'It was okay' or 'I don't recall', or 'Sure was' or 'You got me' or 'I guess' or my personal favorite, 'Is that important?' One thing for sure, Elizabeth 'Bubba' McClain compelled yours truly to tweak his interviewing techniques. And this is her story.

When Dr. John W. McClain made house calls in Mitchell County, GA, his vivacious daughter Elizabeth would dash to the barn so she could turn the starting crank handle on the family's Model T Ford then jump in the driver's seat to putt-putt from the barn to the front porch of the farm house where her father patiently awaited. She said, "The other town doctor in Pelham wouldn't make a house call if he was playing a game of Bridge, so my dad got all the business." McClain's grandfather was also a doctor. Elizabeth stated, "I knew by the 5th grade I'd either be a missionary or a nurse; it's sort of the family thing to do."

Major Bubba, as she is called, recalled that during The Great Depression her father received payments for medical services with chickens, corn, an occasional hog, and on rare occasions, money. Major Bubba said, "We grew vegetables and mother made lye soap in the backyard. All of us knew the country was in the grips of a major depression, but my family was lucky. We had plenty of food, clothes on our backs, and a roof over our heads." Asked about her nickname, she said, "The little girl down the road was a bit 'slow' with word pronunciation, so she called my grandfather 'Doc' and my father 'Doctor Me Doc;' she called my mother 'McMomma' and always called me 'Bubba'. I don't know why; I mean, I never chewed tobacco or drove a pickup truck."

Sparsely populated, the central gathering place in the small town of Pelham was a four-storied building called the Hand Trading Company. Major Bubba recalled, "It served as our post office, grocery store, drug store, a funeral home, and hardware store, a clothing store, and a few other things. One of my brothers delivered mail from Hand Trading in a horse and buggy."

After high school graduation in 1929, Major Bubba stayed in Pelham to study advanced curriculums in biology and chemistry while tending her elderly parents. When her six siblings finally took over parental care, Major Bubba moved to Atlanta in 1939 for nursing courses at the old Piedmont Hospital on Capital Avenue. In her second year of studies, pilots of the Rising Sun paid a surprise visit to Pearl Harbor.

"I was in downtown Atlanta shopping at Davison's Department Store when someone announced Pearl Harbor had just been bombed," she recalled. "I don't recall what all the customers were saying but I knew America was at war. Within just a few days, an Army nurse spoke to our graduating class. I liked what she had to say, so I joined up."

As a licensed registered nurse, Major Bubba sidestepped basic training and received a commission as 2nd Lieutenant on September 05, 1942. "They sent me to Camp Wheeler, Georgia for my first assignment," she stated. "Most of the soldiers had been hospitalized for heat related problems during their training." After two years at Camp Wheeler, Major Bubba received orders for Fort McPherson, Georgia where she served for three more years. "I was at Fort McPherson when the war ended," she recalled. "At Fort Mac we treated combat veterans as well as boys hospitalized for other illnesses."

Major Bubba decided to stay in the Army after WWII. When asked why she chose a career in the military, she stated, "It just seemed like the right thing to do." Asked if she enjoyed the Army, she replied, "Well, I'm not sorry I went in." When asked about Army food, she said, "Well, I ate it."

After a three year stint at Fort McPherson, her next port-of-call was the devastated 'Pearl of the Orient' city of Manila in the Philippines. Sailing aboard a ship out of San Francisco, Major Bubba recalled, "We crossed the Pacific Ocean. That sure was a long voyage and we were glad to see land, but after we docked in Manila we were told some of the nurses would stay in the Philippines and the rest of us were bound for Okinawa. One nurse pitched a temper tantrum about going to Okinawa so I resolved the issue by volunteering to take her place. Boy, what a mistake that was."

Okinawa proved to be a miserable 18 month assignment for Major Bubba. "I didn't like the typhoons," she complained. "I absolutely hated Okinawa. One typhoon made landfall and destroyed half of our barracks. That didn't upset me so much since I bunked in the other half, but the next day it reversed course and hammered Okinawa again; destroying my half of the barracks. I hated Okinawa!"

Obviously unsettled with bad memories, we moved on with the interview to her next port-of-call, Fort Jay on Governor's Island, New York. "I loved Fort Jay," she commented with an enormous grin. "Fort Jay was wonderful duty. I would not have complained one bit had the Army let me stay there for the rest of my career." When asked what was so special about Fort Jay, she replied, "It wasn't on Okinawa!"

Future postings included Hot Springs, Arkansas, Frankfurt, Germany, and a final five years of her career at Fort Eustis, VA. Major Elizabeth "Bubba" McClain retired from the U.S. Army in December of 1962. She returned home to Pelham, GA to tend to family business then moved in with her three sisters in Atlanta. Together the four McClain sisters nurtured two ailing brothers-in-law and in due course, each other. Bubba McClain has been a resident of Morningside Assisted Living in Conyers since 2009.

During the interview, McClain stated, "During the war when I was at Camp Wheeler, a young nurse came into the ward and noticed a black soldier in one of the beds. She said, 'What's he doing in here?' The soldier pointed at me and said, 'She knows.' I told that bratty young nurse, 'Listen here, this man is my patient, he's an American soldier, and you can just vamoose!' Well, she skedaddled, and I was glad that she did. What she said wasn't right, so I assigned her to bed pan duty."

Major Elizabeth 'Bubba' McClain was born on January 11, 1912. She slipped gently into the good night on October 31, 2011, 73 days shy of her 100th birthday. She never married.

Kathleen Eidson
The Fairest One Of All

"I celebrated my 97th birthday this past September," she proclaimed with a huge grin. Then in a robust voice belted-out, '*Sometimes I grew weary and wearier, and life became dreary and drearier, but then I was told, you're not getting old; you're just chronologically* superior.' And it's nice to be superior in at least one category, don't you think?"

Kathleen Eidson (Ejdson in her native Norwegian) conveys superiority in the noblest category of all: that of a first-class human being. Kathleen is also a United States Marine.

The small town of Coffeeville, Alabama received the youngest of ten Eidson children into its community on September 15, 1919, on the same day her oldest brother, also a Marine, came home from The Great War, better known as World War One. The little girl's name was Kathleen. One of her sisters later served as a Lieutenant in the Army Nurse Corps and a brother, Tom, lost his life as a Captain on Anzio Beach in the spring of 1944.

Kathleen's physician father passed away when she was six years old. She said, "We moved to LaGrange, Georgia in 1925. One of my brothers worked as the high school principal then accepted a position at the Atlanta Boy's High School. So we all moved to Atlanta to keep the family together. I was 15 years old when I graduated from the Atlanta Girl's High School." Kathleen found employment at a local bank.

She recalled her decision to join the Marines. "I decided it was my time to do my part for the war effort after my brother, Tom, lost his life on Anzio Beach. Plus, since my oldest brother was a Marine in World War One and lived his life by the creed 'once a Marine, always a Marine,' I admired him and wanted to be like him. I enlisted in February of 1945 in the United States Marine Corps Women Reserves, called the USMCWR. We enlisted for the duration of the war."

Twenty six year old Kathleen Eidson traveled by train to Camp Lejeune, North Carolina. "I thought Camp Lejeune was gigantic," she recalled. "It certainly gave me an insight into military service. In due course I was assigned as a paymaster because of my background in banking." When asked about her conversion to military life, Kathleen replied, "Well, you learn to live by a timetable and answer the call to duty each morning when a bugle sounds reveille or when they play the colors. We slept in bunk beds, and you'd better be sure a quarter could bounce off your sheets in the morning after you made your bed."

On auxiliary assignments: "I had to clean the Head (latrine). That included the open shower stalls and the 'facilities' that were not open for public viewing. One time I came back from my paymaster duties to find my name listed for EPD, which meant 'extra police duty'. I was in trouble; the Head had not passed inspection because a bar of soap was in a shower soap holder. Well, I knew something was wrong but when the drill instructor asked me, 'Do you have an excuse, private?' Of course I answered, "No excuse, sir!" That was always the official response. Another Marine had returned from mess duty and took a shower after I had cleaned and inspected the Head, but you don't rat on your group. You accept the discipline and work as a team because a team has more influence than a single individual. Anyway, I picked up cigarette butts around the area for over a week."

When asked her opinion on Marine Corps drill instructors, she crooned another ditty, "*His voice is rough, he's tough and gruff, he calls us down when we strut our stuff, and he's salty, oh me, oh my, the D.I. from P.I.* (Paris Island)." Then she added, "We considered the D.I.s to be in a class by themselves. One time a new D.I. came in for training by the older D.I. The younger D.I. lined us up and kept demanding 'Heads up, shoulders back, step out!' The older D.I. just kept watching. The new D.I. said things like, 'Number three, step forward, now, number eight, step back a little,' in his way of thinking we just didn't line up properly. The old D.I. finally told him, 'Line them up and gaze down their backs, not their fronts, and they will be in proper order.' You see, some of us lady Marines were more gifted in certain areas than others so there was no way to line up perfectly in front."

On military chow: "I thought it was good. I remember the first time we went to mess. I got my food and took the tray to a table, sat down, and ate at my normal pace. Well, I finished and looked around. Patrol 45, my unit, was gone. I hustled outside and there they were, all lined up waiting for me. I just stood there as they started singing, *'Here we stand like birds in the wilderness, waiting for our chow hound.'* From then on I was never the last one out of the mess hall."

Kathleen observed combat training, hand to hand fighting, the use of a flame thrower, and a wide variety of weapon demonstrations. "We ran an obstacle course but it sure wasn't as challenging as the men's course. After completing the six week basic training course, I stayed on as paymaster but several of the girls fell into jobs normally held by male Marines. You see, early in the war, lady Marines could only be assigned about 20 different duties, but by 1945 female Marines held down over 300 types of work so more males would be freed up for the final push of the war."

Kathleen's remarks on the trials and tribulations of lady Marines: "Well, the Base Commandant ordered that the male Marines weren't to use any sort of 'cutsie' acronyms for lady Marines, but every day going back to the barracks some smart mouth would make a noise like a rocket, one for each lady Marine, like this, 'Fire one, Fire two...fuueee-www...BAM!' Well, we thought BAM meant Beautiful American Marine; in fact it meant Broad Ass Marine. We protested to the camp newspaper and they printed an article about how male Marines should respect us for holding down jobs so the men could go fight. They claimed we were essential to the war effort and we performed our jobs commendably. The paper said we were WR's, which meant Women Reserves.

Well, the very next Monday my friend and I were walking back to our barracks when suddenly we heard, 'Fire one, Fire two...fuueeww-www...BAM!' Another Marine told his buddy, 'Hey, we can't do that anymore. We're supposed to call them WR's.' The smart mouth replied, 'Well, it's the same thing, Wide Rear-ends.' Sometimes you just can't win, although we called the men HAMs, which meant Hairy Ass Marines."

Corporal Kathleen Eidson was discharged in June, 1946. She worked less than a month for the same bank then accepted a position with the Lathem Time Corporation as Company Comptroller. She retired as Vice-President of Finance after 37 years.

Kathleen is an affiliate of the Women Marine Association, she's addressed the Georgia legislature, and sings with a Lady Marines Glee Club called the 'Sometimes Singers'. Of the 'Sometimes Singers' she chanted, *"We will sing for thee, sometimes, even sing on key, sometimes, when the notes you hear fall on your ear, we will bring you cheer, sometimes."*

She entertains at adult centers, civic organizations, AARP gatherings, and considers herself a professional 'Humorist-Story Teller.' Her viewpoint: *"Live Happily Ever Laughter."* Kathleen writes original poetry plus instructs classes at the Senior University of Greater Atlanta at Mercer University and the Emory University Academy of Retired Professionals. Her motto: "We don't stop laughing because we grow old; we grow old because we stop laughing."

Kathleen has climbed the Great Wall of China, piloted a hot air balloon over Kenya's Serengeti, took a month long cruise to Tahiti on a cargo freighter, shot the Chattahoochee River in a one-girl raft, and has the bragging rights for visiting all 50 states and all seven continents.

"I love people," she stated. "And I love to laugh, and I love people with a sense of humor. A lady without a tooth in her head from Cabbage Town once told me, 'I guess I'm at that awkward age in a woman's life; too young for Medicare and too old for men-to-care.' What a lovely sense of humor that lady had."

A passionate Methodist, a patriot, and a great American, Kathleen broke into another melody she composed before the interview concluded: *"When I was in boot camp, I really was slimmer; with marching and workouts my figure was trimmer. But now that I'm older, I face a dilemma, because I am no longer fair.*

"When I was in boot camp, the men were attentive; to ward off their passes took measures inventive. Now getting an escort, I need an incentive, because I am no longer fair.

"When I was in boot camp, a cute smile I crinkled; now all of my facial and neck skin is wrinkled. My once raven tresses with gray hairs are sprinkled, and so I am no long fair."

I disagree. This author had the honor and privilege to meet and interview the fairest one of all: U.S. Marine Corporal Kathleen Eidson.

Marie Mason
Helping Others For Over One Hundred Years

Swan Quarter, NC has a population of 324 according to the 2019 census. The tiny town sits at an elevation of 2' and is bestowed a ranking as the 22,512th largest city in America. Two landing docks offered access to the Atlantic Ocean via Swan Quarter Bay into Pamlico Sound, after which Salt-Life aficionados have to transverse a selection of channels through a string of barrier reefs. You fuel your vehicles at Pat's Service Station. Newman Seafood and Hobo Seafood offered a fresh catch or quick meal in days gone by, but an internet search today warns hungry travelers, *'We're sorry, Swan Quarter doesn't have any restaurants.'* Rural as that may sound, contemplate the comforts Swan Quarter offered, or didn't offer, in 1916.

Marie Mason was born into a farming family five miles from the settlement of Swan Quarter in 1916. She grew up with two sisters and four brothers, all with daily chores to help run a family farm of milk cows, chickens, hogs, plus crops of soy and corn. A bright, free-spirited young woman, Marie graduated high school at age 16, finished nursing school in 1937, earned an Associate Degree in 1941, received a BA Degree in 1947, earned a Masters of Arts in Sociology and Counseling in 1949, and finished a Doctorate in Philosophy in 1966. Dedicated to 'helping others', Marie retired in 1998 at the young-at-heart age of 82. Still spry and living at home, she recently celebrated her 100th birthday. As she conceded on July 23, 2016, "I didn't mind being 99, but 100 is really old!" And this is her story.

A very brief outline of her civilian life: Marie's older sister was her 7th grade teacher in an old two-room schoolhouse. With no available employment opportunities, Marie vamoosed Swan Quarter after high school graduation to enter nursing school. With diploma in hand, she worked as the head nurse on night duty at a large hospital. She attended Campbell University at age 23, worked as the school nurse for free tuition, played on the girls' basketball team, and during her third year took over as coach and director of physical education. In 1941, she decided to stay on at Campbell as a full time nurse, director of PE, and basketball coach.

December 7, 1941: "We were tossing horseshoes when we got the news about Pearl Harbor. We were furious and wondered why they did

.t to us. All the boys were gone, no boys on the campus after Pearl Harbor. My youngest brother joined up and piloted B-17s. I was worried about who'd take care of him if injured, then I thought, '*Well, why not me?' I'm a nurse.*' So I joined up." (Marie's youngest brother flew bomber missions deep into Germany, including Berlin. At war's end, he was the only surviving crew member).

After the war, Marie resumed studies at Meredith College, got her B.A., and worked at various hospitals, including St. Joseph, Good Samaritan, and Central Baptist. She became director of nursing at Kentucky Baptist and later attended the University of Kentucky for three years. In 1950, she married John Mason. She stated, "I don't know why we married. I didn't love him and he didn't love me. We never lived together much; he worked a job in Detroit and came home on the weekends. We stuck it out for 15 years then divorced in 1965."

In 1965, Marie accepted an appointment as the Dean of Students at Meredith College. "I did not enjoy being Dean," she said. "You had to put up with drama queen parents; deal with the panty raids by the boys from NC State up the road, unravel the tribulations of faculty, parents, students, teachers…it was the worst job I ever had!"

An excerpt from Marie via the Women's Veterans Historical Project/ Oral History: "I often tell people that I'm so thankful for my training and my education. I went into nursing. If I never made a penny nursing then I understood my body and how it works or how it doesn't work. And then I went into psychology, so I know my hang-ups and what I can do about them. I know other people's hang-ups, if they would do something about that (laughter). So I learned my body and I learned my mind."

At one hundred years of age, one's memory has a bad habit of fading a bit during an interview. I've taken the liberty to add extracts from Mrs. Mason's bio and her interview with the Women Veterans Historical Project Oral History to fill in overlooked info.

The catalyst for Marie's transition of understanding was a global struggle called World War II. A farmer's daughter, a hometown girl prone to homesickness, driven to helping others and to serve her country, pinned on the butter bars of a 2nd Lt. then boarded a converted luxury liner that zig-zagged across The Pond to avoid German submarines. After a short-lived docking in North Africa, Marie sailed on to the 262nd Station Hospital 30 miles north of Naples, Italy. The horrors of war awaited her.

In her own words: "The sun was coming up as we left New York Harbor. I saluted the Statue of Liberty, and said, '*Dear Lady, I sure hope I see you again.*' Well, I never did because I came home from the other side. I stayed in Italy for three years. We took care of the boys from Anzio Beach. The surgeons operated all night on these boys, terrible wounds. I was assigned to the ward next to surgery, none of them recovered, no one survived. I stayed with them as they expired and thought how these boys would want their parents or a family member with them at the end. But it was only me.

"Our hospital was in a little town called Aversa, north of Naples in what's called the Boot of Italy. A POW camp was across the street from us, mostly Germans and a few sick Russians. Those guys didn't get along very well, but we treated both.

"The first Germans we treated were SS officers, very rude, very nasty men who disrespected female officers. But that didn't last long. We started receiving German soldiers as young as 14 plus old men unfit for combat. They kept saying, '*We don't like this war; we didn't want this war.*' Our boys didn't like the war either. Most of the emotionally ill came from Anzio Beach, just boys whose hair had already turned white. When an air raid siren sounded those poor boys would run, just run, anywhere, and I'd have to go after them. One time during a raid a piece of shrapnel landed in front of me, not 6" away, so I was that close. I picked it up and hid it in my duffle bag.

"We treated a wide range of injuries, including buttocks. We treated a lot of buttocks, you know, guys would sit on a land mine or catch shrapnel in their buttocks, buttocks all torn to pieces, buttocks exposed to you daily. We learned how to graft skin, but more serious cases went to a general hospital.

"Sometimes we ran out of food; we ran out of supplies, we had to make do. I also had duty in the psychiatric ward. The soldiers in there were alive but just out of this world as they could be. German planes would strafe, too. They'd strafe the main road then turn over our hospital which was clearly marked with the Red Cross, but they kept their guns firing so ended up strafing the hospital.

"I also had six wards filled with soldiers who had contacted some type of venereal disease from Italian women. I gave them their penicillin shots with the biggest syringe I could find and a bunch of sterile needles. I told them, '*When you hear me coming, pull your pajamas down and roll over on your bellies. I'm not going to stand here and wait for you because I have a hundred of you to do.*' So, I'd shoot one, replace the needle, shoot another one then continue on down the line. There was a kid in there, very young soldier; he asked for the most ragged needle we had for his last shot before being discharged. When I asked him why, he replied, '*I'm going to put it in my pocket, and when I start to do something I shouldn't, I am going to look at that needle!*' (Laughs)

"You know, my mother died in 1940 and I left college to take care of my father, but he told me, 'No, you go back and finish your schooling. You have a life to live, so go on back.' Well, I did, but my father died in 1944 while I was in Italy. I received no letters and had no contact with my family while in Italy. My brother, Clyde, called the Red Cross to hopefully find me and give me the bad news. They told him they could not tell him where I was, but that I was okay. They at least told me he had called them.

"Oh, I forgot to mention…after the invasion of Southern France they'd send captive Germans to us for treatment. We'd get a call about how many Germans were on the plane. Well, on one flight we expected 15 but only 14 got off the plane. When we asked about the missing German, we were informed he became unruly during the flight so they tossed him out. I couldn't have done that, but our combat soldiers ... well, you just didn't pester them."

The war in Europe was over; Marie and her nurses were going home, or so they thought. She recalled, "MacArthur needed experienced nurses for the upcoming invasion of Japan, so we headed for the Pacific. We went through the Panama Canal and a Navy band was playing for us. We booed them. They thought we were crazy, but we kept booing. We wanted to go home! We were allowed off the ship to buy fresh fruit. Shouldn't have. All of us ended up with diarrhea."

Halfway across the Pacific, Marie and her nurses received the news that two new type of bombs, atomic bombs, had been dropped on Japan ... that war, too, was over. "We were so happy," she said. "We knew we were going home so we tossed our duffle bags over the side of the ship. We were, in fact, continuing on to the Philippines. When they found out we'd deep-sixed our duffle bags, we almost received a court martial. Anyway, when we arrived in the Philippines you couldn't see anything but ships, ships as far as the eye could see, all gathered for the massive invasion of Japan. I don't think I would have survived that invasion, had it taken place.

"Well, we ended up camping out in a rice paddy for three months with nothing to do. We'd hitch a ride on a native motorcycle to visit Manila, but there wasn't too much left of that city. The corpsmen and doctors were sent to Japan, but we nurses boarded one of our hospital ships and sailed home. I brought home a horrid souvenir, a horrible case of jungle rot, my face, hands, arms, chest, were just about raw. I was a pretty sight."

WWII was over. Marie returned to school, nursing, and marriage in 1950. Marie and her husband applied for a G.I. Home Loan which was refused with the statement, *'You can't have a loan. You'll get pregnant and will never pay us back.'*

Another story from Italy: "We took a tour of the Vatican in Rome and guess who we ran into? The Pope! The Catholic nurses took out their rosaries and let me borrow one, then the Pope blessed each and every one of us and our rosaries. Pretty funny, considering that I'm a Baptist."

When asked if she'd do it all over again, she replied, "I was proud to have served my country and contribute to the war effort. War is horrible, but, yes, you bet'cha, I would do it all over again, but I wouldn't throw my gear overboard."

The significance of 'The Greatest Generation' has one of its best exemplars in Marie Mason. God bless the nurses.

Dorothy Turner
The Riveter Vs. Dorothy The Welder

I first met Dorothy Turner while conducting an interview with another WWII female veteran at Morningside Assisted Living Facility in Conyers, Georgia. At first I thought the woman shy; but that turned out to be a great big joke, because once Dorothy started talking you shut-up, sat back, and listened. She spoke with authority; she spoke the truth; she expected to be heard; Dorothy sounded like a United States Marine. A couple of days later I received a call from her son, Dan Turner.

Dan asked if I'd be interested in interviewing a WWII Marine, his mother, Dorothy Turner. He did stipulate a few necessary rules: Do not provoke her, do not disrespect her, and don't try to sweet-talk her unless you aspired to have the holy crap beat out of you. The interview sounded refreshing, to say the least.

I interviewed Dorothy in her modest room at Morningside with Dan sitting next to his mother in case the need arose for recall assistance or statement clarification. Well, that's the second great big joke. Dorothy was the one that corrected both of us, more than once.

Cursed with the aches and pains attributed to the Golden Years, Dorothy's razor-sharp cognizance and clever critique remained intact. She was blunt, not of rudeness, but of a woman trained as a Marine with no time for poppycock. Her values were that of a Marine, and she expected respect be given for the respect she tendered.

Her husband served in WWII as a Navy Seabee at locations few Americans had ever heard about until the victories and casualties on remote shores became front page headlines, battlefields like the Aleutian Islands and Guadalcanal. Dorothy became a Gold Star mother during the Vietnam War when her son Michael lost his life in the critical combat for the ancient city of Hue during the 1968 Tet Offensive. Michael had been 'in-country' only one week.

Dorothy's Marine photo displayed on a wall in her living room portrayed an attractive, young, patriotic woman with a smile to delight any man. Yet the Golden Years had taken their toll, raiding her beauty and her youth, but not that beautiful smile, her dignity, nor her stature as a United States Marine.

> *"A woman is the only thing I am afraid of*
> *that I know will not hurt me."*
> — **Abraham Lincoln**

Obviously Honest Abe never met Dorothy.

Dan Turner is always apprehensive when he receives a call from the staff at Morningside Assisted Living Facility. His mom, Dorothy Turner, resides at the facility and has not been in the best of health as of late.

Dan said, "I received a call one evening from Morningside and was told I'd better get out there as quickly as possible. When I asked what was wrong, they told me, 'The Marines have landed at Morningside, bunches of them!' Knowing mom, that didn't really surprise me." Before participating in a surprise Marine invasion of Morningside, Dorothy had quite a life, but not a quiet life. She liked it that way.

Opha Mae Johnson got the ball rolling for lady Marines on August 13, 1918 when she enlisted during WWI for clerical responsibilities. During WWII, 23,000 women served as lady Marines in a wide variety of assignments. By the end of the war, 85% of all enlisted USMC personnel assigned to headquarters were women.

Cpl. Dorothy Turner, USMC, was one of those very few, the proud, the lady Marines of WWII.

Born and raised in the Land of Lincoln, Dorothy mastered numerous male-dominated skills as a young woman, such as plumbing, welding, and riveting. She said, "My father was a teamster truck driver in the good old days. I danced many a tune with teamster boss Jimmy Hoffa." But Dorothy complained that her father would find out every time she went 'juking' with friends. "I would always be spotted by a trucker if I snuck out and went nightclubbing and he'd tattletale to my father! It just didn't seem fair."

Dorothy wanted to join the Marine Corps before the outbreak of WWII and asked her father's permission. She said, "My father said…well, I can't really tell you what my father said, but it meant 'No'!"

Her father's firm 'NO' didn't hold back Dorothy for long. When she heard on a car radio that the Japanese had bombed Pearl Harbor, she joined the Marines immediately, without her father's approval. When asked what her father said when she informed him of her enlistment, Dorothy replied, "Well, there you go again. To be honest, I can't really tell you what dad said, not without sounding too unlady-like."

Sent to Camp Lejeune, Dorothy spent the war doing what she mastered as a young woman: plumbing, welding, and riveting. She said with a smile, "Rosie the Riveter was a pushover; the hard-hitting lady in the crowd was Dorothy the Welder."

Hard-hitting perfectly depicted Dorothy Turner. Loyal, hard-working and independent, she nonetheless dodged a court-martial. She explained the incident, "I was sound asleep one morning when the barracks sergeant came in and whacked me on my foot to wake me up. That was a huge mistake on her part. I came up swinging and knocked the woman out cold." Albeit, a court-martial never materialized due to the fact Dorothy's enlistment records clearly indicated, 'she hates to be rudely awakened.'

Her son Dan confirmed the trait. "I learned at an early age how to wake up Mom. Tap her on the arm and run like hell!"

Dorothy met her husband, Bud, on a blind date. Dorothy said, "Bud was a Navy Seabee in WWII. The Seabee's were the first to land on Guadalcanal so Bud placed a sign on the beach that said, 'Welcome, U.S. Marines.' According to Bud, the Marines failed to see the humor."

Her husband also served in the Aleutians where he met a young soldier from Georgia named Charles West, son of George West, proprietor of the West Lumber Company and the First Federal Savings and Loans. Dorothy stated, "Now you know how we ended up in Georgia. We came south after the war to help George build homes in Atlanta until my husband branched out on his own."

The mother of four boys and one girl, Dorothy became a Gold Star mother during the Vietnam War when her son, Marine Private 1st Class Michael Barry Turner, was killed in action during the Communist Tet Offensive of 1968. Michael had been in Nam only a week when he lost his life in the brutal battle to retake the ancient city of Hue. He was 19 years old.

In their son's honor, Bud and Dorothy Turner established the Michael Barry Turner Memorial Scholarship program in 1969 which lasted for 10 years. The scholarship program awarded three scholarships a year in sports, academics, and music to Towers High School in Decatur, GA. Bud also coached the Midway Mighty Mites football team in order to mentor and help young men get off on the right foot in life.

For over 60 years Dorothy bought and distributed gifts to needy children during the Marine's annual Christmas event, Toys for Tots. If she required assistance with distribution or loading, Dorothy drove to the local Marine recruitment office, marched in and thundered, "You, you, and you, get out here, right now! I need your help." The recruiters never bickered with Dorothy.

Her son, Dan, recalled, "When I was just a young sprout, Dad owned a couple of nightclubs around Atlanta. If the piano player ....."

Dorothy quickly interrupted, "Those weren't nightclubs; they were damn strip joints! I never did like those hoochie-coochie joints."

Dan cleared his throat. "Well, at any rate, if the piano player didn't show up Dad would come get me and we'd sneak off to the club. I'd sit behind the upright piano, sort of out of sight, and played music all night long with some of the best jazz players in Atlanta. I was only nine years old when I first started and didn't get caught by the police until I was 12. Mom never knew about it or she would have killed both of us."

When I asked Dorothy if she ever found out her adolescent son was playing music in strip joints, she replied, "Yeah, Dan finally confessed when he was old enough to outrun me."

When one of her four sons and/or their friends misbehaved or affronted teachers at Glenhaven Elementary School, Dorothy got a call from the school principal, basically hollering for Marine reinforcements to manage disciplinary problems. Dan clarified, "Mom would march to school and haul an unruly son and his friend out into the hallway and blister their butts. Nobody complained back in those days, no lawsuits, no child abuse; nothing but good old-fashioned punishment from an upset and tenacious parent. And, of course, nobody wanted to mess with mom."

Dan recalled numerous times in grocery stores when a rowdy kid was in the checkout line. "Mom would say, 'Lady, either get that child under control or I will!' The disorderly kid would take one look at Mom and settle his butt down, like immediately."

When I asked her to tell a secret or two about Lady Marines, Dorothy stated, "Well, I can't do that, because if I told you the secrets they wouldn't be secrets anymore, now would they?"

On September 9, 2011, the Marine Corp League Devil Dogs Detachment #952 from Duluth, GA along with the General Ray Davis Marine Corp League Detachment #1188 from Monroe, GA, plus over 100 friends, family, community leaders and Morningside residents joined in a celebration of life for U.S. Marine Dorothy Turner. A reenactment of the flag-raising on Iwo Jima closed out the ceremony.

During the celebration, a young lady asked Dorothy, "So, Mrs. Turner, you were a Marine in WWII?" Dorothy cut her eyes at the woman and replied with authority, "No, young lady, I *am* a Marine!"

On Oct 22, 2011, United States Marine Dorothy Turner departed this life and immediately marched up to and through the entrance to the Pearly Gates. The thunderclap created when the gates slammed against the backstops was heard worldwide. Saint Peter said nary a word.

Alice Stallings
Her Hair In Rollers And Wearing Red Fuzzy-Wuzzy Houseshoes

The Yellow Brick Assisted Living Home in Lithonia, GA echoes with the good ghosts of a good history. My wife's childhood physician, Dr. Stewart, operated his family practice from the basement where Joyce was allowed to play with the medical instruments that helped establish her lifelong interest in medicine. Dr. Stewart's medical instruments are still on display in the upstairs parlor, including his 'Birthing Book' with the birth date of my wife's kid sister, Carole.

Amy Brown, the social director, introduced Ralph Way and Alice Stallings as we gathered in the front room parlor. Listening to these two wonderful people of the Greatest Generation reminded me of a George Burns and Gracie Allen routine, hilarious, yet filled with the wisdom and wit conveyed from the hard knocks and pleasurable moments in life.

Ralph, born in 1922 in St. George, South Carolina, said of Georgia and North Carolina, "Shoot, as far as we were concerned those were foreign countries." Alice, born in 1919, said of her hometown Carlton, GA, "It wasn't much more than a little wide place in the road." As survivors of the Great Depression, they recognized the value of a good job and hard work; as witnesses to WWII, they understood the magnitude of a great country and the true cost of freedom.

Ralph joined the Army Air Corps before the outbreak of war in June of 1941. Stationed at Maxwell Field, AL, he was relaxing without a care in the world on the steps of the state capitol in Montgomery on December 7, 1941. Ralph recalled, "A police car drove by announcing over a loudspeaker that Japanese aircraft had bombed Pearl Harbor. I dashed back to base as fast as I could, knowing my life had changed forever."

Alice recalled, "It was like yesterday. We were all coming out of church when the service station boy came running up to us saying Pearl Harbor had been bombed. My husband had graduated from the Upton Jones Military School, so I knew he'd be going in." Asked if her husband had joined or been drafted, Alice replied, "He was drafted. If he had joined, I would have killed him."

Ralph, a trained airplane mechanic and flight engineer, said of the time, "I knew my next port-of-call would be smack dab in the middle of a combat zone, so volunteered for overseas duty." He was turned down three times. "Shoot, I gave up after the third refusal and kept working on C-46s and C-47s." Three weeks after the third re-jection, Ralph's 1st Sergeant called him into his office and said, 'Bad news, Ralph, they're sending you into combat.' Ralph said, "I didn't do nothing but smile. That's the Army for you." He was sent with nine other men to Miami, Florida, bedecked in dress wool uniforms.

"Good Lord, it was hot," he said. "I was placed in quarantine be-cause I needed another shot, but after two weeks I was put on a cargo plane as its only passenger heading for Karachi, India. Thing was, the darn plane wouldn't start." The plane finally 'fired-up' at 2:00 am the next morning. Ralph recalled, "I wasn't too confident that plane could make it all the way to Karachi, but we finally landed there four days later."

Ralph claimed his war was not of glory and glamour but of hard work and endless apprehension that the cargo planes he maintained would make it over 'The Hump'—The Himalayan Mountain Range—into China. "We lost hundreds of cargo planes flying over The Hump," he said. "That's a little known sacrifice our brave flyers made that history seems to have forgotten." Eventually, Ralph was given an alleged vaca-tion, a one week visit to a rest camp in the mountains of Afghanistan. "That's where I picked up Myrtle," he said with a grin. Asked about the woman, Ralph said, "Myrtle wasn't a lady, she was an orphaned mon-key." Myrtle the Monkey slept and ate with Ralph and his roommate. "She liked my roommate's cigarettes, ate them like candy." Asked what happened to Myrtle, Ralph said, "We had to give her to another soldier when we left. Who knows, maybe they got married." Ralph received a monthly military check for $21.00. After the war, he attended Clemson University and had a long successful career in Insurance.

While stationed in Alabama, Ralph met his future wife, Ange-lina, but before the relationship really took hold, Ralph was sent overseas. "We corresponded throughout the war but you know how those things go. She was a very intelligent woman, graduated from

Montevallo College then attended Emory University where she earned a Master's in Library Science. I couldn't wait to get home and break her ribs with a hug." Albeit, as 'those things go', the reunion was a bit awkward, both not knowing where they stood with each other. "We, uh, well, we sort of shook hands," he said. Handshakes work: Ralph and Angelina were married for 62 years until her passing.

Alice Cooper and James Stallings exchanged wedding vows on June 22, 1941 in the old Baptist Church in Lithonia, Georgia. "My husband's family and Senator Max Cleland's family were neighbors," she said. "You should have seen the turnout for our wedding. We were poor as a pair of church mice, but the Presbyterian and Methodist preachers knew us and let their congregations out early that Sunday to attend our wedding. Boy, what a party!" The newlyweds had 14 months together before James was drafted. He spent the next three years in the Army Medical Corps treating wounded and dying men.

"James never talked about the war," she said. "He'd mention humorous episodes but never the horrible injuries he saw and treated." What Alice did know of James' tour included mobile medical assignments in the thick of epic battles for North Africa, France, and Germany. "He stated his duties required him to do what doctors do today," she said.

Corresponding via V-mails, the heavily censored letters at least kept the couple in touch. "We would number the letters so we knew which ones to open and read first," Alice recalled. Injured soldiers sent to Atlanta medical facilities to recover from their wounds would call Alice with news of James and she'd go visit the boys. Alice said, "That's the least I could do for them."

Alice held down the home front while James treated casualties across The Pond. "I bought a business called Nifty Beauty Shop across the street from Gailey's Shoes in Old Town Conyers. During the war the textile mill in Milstead operated 24/7 so the women working the early shift would call to make 6:00am appointments. That was okay with me; I didn't have anything else to do." The price for a half-perm: $ 3.00. A full perm cost $5.00. No tips, that was unheard of. Alice said, "I knew everything going on in this county. Wet a woman's hair and she'll tell you anything."

Her tenant across the upstairs landing was attorney and future judge, Clarence Vaughn. "Clarence and I would always have our heads stuck out the door every time we heard the mailman," she recalled.

The German surrender ended the fighting in Europe, but a brutal war still raged in the Pacific. James reported to Marseilles, France to await transportation to the Pacific Theater of war in preparation for the invasion of Japan. "He didn't want to go," Alice recalled. "James had seen enough by then, three solid years of death, the dying; the terribly injured. I remember him saying, 'We didn't know what kind of bombs Truman dropped on Japan, but we were sure glad he did.' I was too."

The Second World War was finally over. Alice bought a new dress to greet her returning hero. She said, "I wanted to look pretty for my soldier boy." James showed up one day early. Alice recalled, "He was coming up the stairs, and there I was with my hair in rollers, wearing a white chenille bathrobe with flowery embroidery and a pair of red fuzzy-wuzzy slippers. Shoot, I didn't care; we met halfway down the stairs. And guess what; James didn't care how I looked either!"

Her husband worked until he retired as the Postmaster of Lithonia, Georgia. Alice and James remained together two months short of their 70th wedding anniversary at the time of his passing.

As we closed their interview with small talk, I mentioned that the Greatest Generation of warriors were passing at the rate of one every 90 seconds. Ralph frowned, then said with a big grin, "Shoot, I guess I'd better get back on my vitamins."

June Blasingame Hipps
A Woman's Anguish On The Home Front

June Hipps, in her late 20's, posing in style copy

One of the veterans featured in my first book, *Veterans: Stories From America's Best,* is Iwo Jima survivor Gerald Hipps, better known as "Buddy" to his family and friends. Two of his three sons served in Vietnam. And faithfully awaiting for all of them to return home was wife/mother, June Blasingame Hipps. And this is her story, the anguish of a woman with her men at war, in her own words.

"I was born in Miami, FL in 1928. Buddy (Gerald) and I played together as young kids, both of our grandmothers went to the same church and were good friends. Shoot, our neighborhood was full of kids, we'd play kick the ball, kick the can, things like that. Buddy would visit my home often and I just considered him one of the neighborhood kids. He was a blonde, toe-head kid, a little smart-aleck. His friend, they called him 'Brother', was always hanging around with Buddy."

When did things turn serious?

"Well, my dad gave me a quarter so I could go to the movies on Wednesday, Saturday, and Sunday. I don't know if that was just to get rid of me for a while so he could have some peace and quiet, but he did and I loved the movies and movie stars. So, I'm sitting there in the movies and here comes Buddy and Brother. Buddy sat down beside me and said, 'Mind if I sit beside you?' and I replied, 'You already are.' Then he said, "I'm going to put my arm around you, is that okay?" I replied, 'You don't have to ask me what you're going to do.' I was a smart aleck, too, and came back at Buddy with my own smart aleck remarks.

"After that we'd sit on the porch swing when he came to visit. I really started liking him and he really started liking me. At that time Miami was jam-packed with military guys and I kept on dating for a while, even a classmate from school. Well, Buddy saw me coming from a movie on the bus and he got pretty upset with me. I told him, 'I know the boy; I go to school with him.' But that classmate did not mean anything to me like Buddy did, so from then on Buddy and I dated then married in April of 1946, and we stayed married for 66 years. Buddy lived to be 86 years old and we have had a blessed life, especially with our 32 grandchildren and greatgrandchildren. I keep thinking, shoot, my boys are really vigorous or something like that.'"

Do you recall Pearl Harbor?

"Only vaguely, it was so long ago. Buddy and his good friend, Skeet Shannon, joined the Marines when they were 16 years old, thinking they'd stay together. Buddy's mother had a fit, but he'd already done it so she signed the papers and let him go. He went in at 17, but he and Skeet were soon separated by the Marines. Later in the war, Skeet had a big ship blown out from under him, but he survived the war. Both were in the Marines for three and a half years. We all kept in touch and when Buddy got out of the Marines he started seeing me again, that was in January of 1946. My daddy said, 'No, you're too young', I was about 15 or 16, but he liked Buddy from day one and allowed us to sit on the porch. The porch was where we dated for a long time. Then on April 21, 1946, Buddy said, 'Can we get married?' So, we did, we were married at home. My grandmother invited all the church members and my mom and dad fixed us a big dinner and had people come over. We just had a good old fashioned at-home wedding."

Did Buddy ever talk about Iwo Jima?

"No, never. I didn't know anything about Iwo Jima. The only thing I knew was at night he would struggle, he was fighting, throwing his arms and legs, I thought 'what is wrong with Buddy?' We didn't know anything about PTSD back then. He would holler out in Japanese while sleeping…he didn't know a lot of Japanese, but he knew enough to come back at them, like taunting each other. He would be fighting for his life. We were living with my mom and dad, they didn't understand either; it was a bit scary. He thought he saw people outside our windows; he was scared for his life and mine.

"Then we started having children. We had Gary, then two years later we had Terry, then two years later we had Michael. We thought we were so blessed. We stayed with mom and dad for six years and they loved the boys. We bought a G.I. home in Hialeah, FL and that's where we raised our three boys. We would walk down Flagler Street in Miami with the three of them dressed in cowboy uniforms, that was the thing back then, and Terry loved to wear his guns. Very outgoing, thought he was John Wayne, I guess. Gary was more reserved, very quiet, has taken it easy most of his life. Michael was the hell-raiser, he liked attention. Mike was an extrovert, smiling all the time, he always wanted to look good and smell good. He liked nice cologne."

Tell us about Vietnam.

Gary was drafted while in high school and went into the army when he was 19. It broke my heart, I didn't want to see him go. You know, young boys all around us were going to college to avoid the military. Not my boys.

"And just like Gary, when Terry turned 19 he was drafted while in high school. Both had to go.

"Mike comes along two years later, he was too young to be drafted, but he said, 'I can't let my two brothers be over there and I can't go and help, so I'm going to join.' I begged him not to go even though I knew it was the right thing for him to do, but still, I didn't want him to. But he joined, got married, and ended up in Wichita, KS. But his wife couldn't handle military life and couldn't hold down a job if they found out Mike was in the military. So Mike got an honorable discharge and brought her home. She was very young, perhaps 17, and missed her parents and home. She had counseling but that didn't help. Mike did not have to go to Vietnam, although he was scheduled to do so.

So, two out of three sons went to Vietnam?

"Yes. Mike came home from Wichita, Gary was coming home from Vietnam, and Terry was already over there. The day Gary, our first born, left for Vietnam was a heartbreaker. I don't even like to think about it sometimes because I could not face the fact that they could come and say, 'Okay, you have to go into the service.' So there he was in a war, I never knew where Gary was, and it was very frightening. I couldn't visualize my sons in a war. Those were hard times back then, all the boys were leaving for Vietnam. Yet I was very blessed because my three boys came home while so many other mother's sons didn't.

"Gary didn't talk about Vietnam, but he did tell me a story about a little girl who was missing an arm. She was two or three years old and walking down a road to where he and his unit were. Gary knew a lot of them were booby-trapped, that she could have a bomb or grenade on her, but he picked her up and sat by the side of the road and just held her. He said, 'Momma, I cried like a baby. I felt so sorry for her knowing that here is this little child and she's already lost an arm in this terrible war.'

"That's all he told me for years, but not too long ago Gary told me about the good people over there and how they would help American soldiers hide if in danger. They'd hide the soldiers under their houses, but he said, 'I got to thinking, if we can come down here so can the enemy, plus those people were putting their lives in danger because the VC would have shot all of them. Gary and his buddies left the village and made it back to their base. I don't ask my boys about Vietnam, but sometimes I wish they would talk to me or at least go to the VA and get help so they could wipe this stuff out of their minds. But Gary stated, 'Momma, it will never go away.'"

And Terry?

"I remember sitting in the living room one day when a helicopter came over. Terry jumped straight up. I said, 'What's wrong?', and he replied, 'That just brought back memories and it scared the devil out of me.' I knew that Terry was given orders for California to join some Navy personnel although he was in the Army, but never told me anything until that day the helicopter flew over our house. He explained how the helicopters in Vietnam would drop him into a tree then leave him there. He would sit there and radio back enemy activity. I said, 'They could have found you and killed you.' He said, 'Well, I was fortunate, the choppers would eventually come back and get me from behind enemy lines, and sometimes I wasn't even sure where I was.' That's all I know about Terry."

How did you feel when your first born returned?

"I was thrilled to death, and thanked God every day, even today, that my boys got home, even with PTSD, but they are whole, not crippled, didn't lose a limb, but they went through a living hell."

Then Terry went to Vietnam?

"I felt like I'd been through enough, having three sons go into the military in time of war. But I also thought that I was no better than other mothers who sent their sons to war. I didn't have any other choice, that's just the way it was. Another year of anguish. I wrote my boys every day. Terry, like his dad, loved macaroni and cheese. I'd make a huge pot and that was our meal. I couldn't eat it while Terry was in Vietnam, I'd choke on it; I couldn't eat my son's favorite food. (June cried momentarily then she continued) But I was blessed. All my boys made it home. I don't know what they went through, but I can imagine with what their dad went thought on Iwo Jima that they had an awfully hard time, too."

Did the boys write home?

"Yes, but I never knew where they were. We had dinner with Gary's in-laws on New Year's Eve and I told them how much I worried about Gary, but they replied, 'You'd best be worried about Terry, nobody knows where he is.' How they knew that I don't know to this day, but I told them I worried about both my boys. It was not a happy New Year's. I enjoyed them asking us to dinner, but I just couldn't get over the fact that at the time I had two sons in a war and a third scheduled to go. It's a heartbreaker, you're torn apart, but there's nothing you can do. You just have to let them go.

"Even to this day I think about what they may have gone through, but they don't talk about it, they don't tell me anything that bothers them, and I keep saying, 'Tell the VA, tell somebody, even my husband wouldn't talk at first about Iwo Jima. But at the VA clippings started showing up on their bulletin board about Buddy, and one doctor, a wonderful man, finally got Buddy to start talking. Then the VA understood what Buddy had been through so they started posting a lot of things on their bulletin boards. Buddy felt better and he started talking about his time on Iwo Jima to schools or lodges, just about anywhere, but my boys…no. I doubt if they've ever been asked to speak, and I don't think they would accept an invitation to do so."

How did your husband handle Vietnam?

"He was like me, so sad, we tried to make the best of it. We treasured

Mike's time with us, he was the youngest, but when he went in that brought on a total heartbreak. Buddy had been through hell on Iwo Jima, he pretty much knew what they would be going through, but to this day I don't know how we got through it. We just existed, we kept going, built a home, but it was hard knowing those three wonderful boys went to a war straight out of high school."

Tell us about the day all the boys were home.

"Oh, what a wonderful day. I was overjoyed and so was Buddy. They had done a wonderful thing for our country and I wouldn't have expected them to do anything else, but it was very, very difficult. We finally left Florida and moved to Georgia because all my dad's and momma's people were up here. My dad's people were the Blasingames, lived in Monroe and up around that area. My mother was born in Crawfordville. My granddaddy Malcolm owned a large plantation in Crawfordville and was a bookkeeper, just like I was a bookkeeper for the city of Hialeah. My granddaddy was doing very well until the boll weevils came in and wiped him out. From that day on he started drinking, he just couldn't get over it. All my aunts and uncles and cousins were up here around Monroe and Loganville and Winder; that was the best part about living in Florida, being able to take trips up to Georgia to visit family."

Did Buddy like Georgia?

Buddy was ready to move, too. Miami was in transition with the Cubans taking over. They were great neighbors and we liked them, got together often, but it just wasn't the same anymore. You couldn't go into a story without hearing Spanish and my dad said, 'I walk into a store and can't talk to people, I don't know what they're saying and they don't know what I'm saying.' Dad finally moved to Jacksonville. Buddy went through a rough childhood and survived Iwo Jima, he had good times and bad times, but he often said, 'I had a miserable childhood, but I have so much now, I'm thankful, God has let me live,' so he just accepted whatever came his way. Buddy and I worked side by side building this house then all the boys moved up here and worked construction jobs and did very well. Again, Buddy and I were so blessed."

Where are your boys now?

"Gary lives in Monticello, Terry lives in Sparta, Mike lived behind us in a four-car garage apartment until he passed away about 18 months ago from throat cancer. It broke my heart. He always said, 'Mom, you're going to outlive me.' I didn't believe him, but he believed that all his life.

"Ya know, Buddy's best friend Skeet Shannon and his wife live in Middleburg, FL, but I haven't talked to them for over a year and I'm afraid to call them. I don't want to know if they have passed on. They might have because Skeet went blind. But his wife said, 'You wouldn't know he's blind, he's out there planting flowers and doing yard work.' I said, 'That's the Marine in him.' Skeet told me once, 'Marines don't pass away. They just go to hell then come back and regroup.'"

June Blasingame Hipps has had to regroup many times in her 92 years on earth, but she did so with courage, faith, and the determination of a loving wife/mother. She is a living icon of the Greatest Generation.

Ona Lester
Pharmacist's Mate First Class

*"It is not the years in your life but the
life in your years that counts."*
— Adlai Stevenson

The oldest of seven children, Ona Thilla Finseth was born on September 01, 1917 in Byron, Minnesota. She recalled, "I was raised on a chicken and turkey farm. When I attended school we always had prize turkeys for my 4-H projects. Everybody back then had animals on their farms. The Great Depression hurt most people, but my mother told us how lucky we were being farmers. My family didn't go hungry."

She attended school in a one room building heated by a coal stove. "I thought it was modern for the time," Ona stated. "The boys had their own outhouse, and so did the girls." Educational propensity typified the Finseth family—Ona's grandfather was one of the founders of St. Olaf College in Northfield, Minnesota.

Ona remembers the Day of Infamy. "We heard the news on the radio about Pearl Harbor being bombed, then listened to President Roosevelt's famous speech. None of us knew where Pearl Harbor was, but we realized our country was at war."

Leaving Minnesota for the first time, Ona traveled to Washington, D.C. to work for the Treasury Department. After the Treasury Department decentralized, Ona and her job moved to Chicago, Illinois. "I was in Chicago for six months when this girl I worked with said she had joined the WAVES, the women's Navy. I thought, *'Shoot, she wears thick glasses, I don't, if she can get in, so can I',* so I went down to the Merchandise Mart in Chicago and joined the Navy on May 17, 1943."

Sent to Hunter Women's College in New York City for preliminary training, Ona shared a room with a young lady from Iowa until the Navy found out her roommate was underage. "They sent her straight home," Ona said. "Women had to be twenty one, but she was only twenty. So, there I was, in the upper bunk with a room all to myself." With two sisters already in nursing, Ona volunteered for the Navy Hospital Corps. Recalling a plethora of assignments, Ona said, "The Navy shipped me to the Norfolk Naval Hospital in Portsmouth, Virginia, but I mostly did clerical work, including checking officers into the chow hall." Other duties included processing new recruits, but Ona was finally given the opportunity to practice her Hospital Corps training. "I started giving inoculations, but it took me a few sticks to catch-on. The recruits were nice about it, though."

She was promoted to Pharmacist's Mate First Class after supplementary training in Bronx, New York and Bainbridge, Maryland. Proficient in the performance of general hospital duties, Ona worked several positions so males with the rank of Pharmacist Mate First Class could hit the beaches with Marines to render first aid on the battlefield or at a dressing station. "I enjoyed the Navy," Ona said. "It wasn't hard on me at all."

Women in the Hospital Corps normally received a transfer if requested. "I asked for a transfer to the Navy Hospital at Great Lakes, Illinois," she said. "I guess I wanted a different duty." With eye-catching loveliness, when asked if she had the time to socialize while in the military, Ona said, "Well, I was introduced to a nice boy in the hospital, but I found out he was married, so that ended that." Four months later Ona received another transfer to the Navy Personnel Separation Center in Minneapolis, Minnesota. There she helped process sailors out of the Navy—World War Two was finally over, the killing was done. Ona Thilla Finseth received her Honorable Discharge on December 03, 1945.

She met her future husband, Georgia Tech graduate and Naval Lieutenant Barnett Reid Lester, at a Bingo Party in Washington, D.C. They married on November 18, 1950. Ona sewed her own wedding dress. She explained, "The material cost $49.00, including the $10.00 I paid for my veil." Her husband worked for Maryland Light and Power as an engineer until 1974. The Lester's moved to Reid's hometown farm in

Rockdale County, Georgia the same year. Reid worked for the railroad and farmed while Ona settled in as a housewife. Reid passed from this life in 1982.

When asked her first impression of Georgia, Ona said, "Well, it was a lot warmer than Minnesota."

A member of the Greatest Generation, Pharmacist's Mate First Class Ona Thilla Finseth Lester did her part to win the war, and your country thanks you.

Katherine Davis
Proud And Pretty And Patriotic

Grandpas preserve a special place in their hearts for granddaughters, a tender nucleus jammed packed with affection, pride, and above all, protection. Mr. Milt Longbottom is no exception.

I received a lengthy 'kudos' email from Mr. Longbottom expressing appreciation for my articles and how much he enjoyed reading "A Veteran's Story." Then he asked that his granddaughter, Katherine Davis, be considered for an interview. He said that Katherine had served with the United States Marines in Iraq and was willing to convey her story. I answered affirmative within one minute.

Let me be forthright about this: When I served in Vietnam, the U.S. Marine Corps *did not* deploy anything near as attractive as Mr. Longbottom's granddaughter. The Marines I drank with or avoided bar fights with were brutal-looking bipolar alpha males, normally smelly and grimy and spouting lingo too crude for the reading public. The atmosphere given around battle-hardened Marines in Nam intimidated the integrity of the skin around your throat. Admittedly, I never gave the above mentioned criticism to leathernecks in Nam due to a concept called self-preservation.

Ms. Davis is no longer on active duty, but she maintains the sharpness and mannerisms attributed to the USMC. Yes, sirs and no, sirs were cemented into her vocabulary. Cool, calm, cute, and collected, she gave an outstanding interview with perfect articulation. Thankfully my tape was doing its job, because I sat silently captivated listening to a younger generation American warrior and felt a sense of admiration that America still produced men and women of such character, honor, and discipline.

Naturally, the interview was about her. But Marines are not trained as individuals, rather as a Band of Brothers and Sisters that suck it up when needed and put their lives on the line for each other; for you and me, and for the country they took an oath to defend. And above all else, she wanted the phrase 'once a Marine, always a Marine' mentioned in the article. Okay, it has been, but her story need not repeat slogans or phrases to remind us of the Marine Corps' proud history. In my humble opinion the Iwo Jima monument in Washington, DC and untold thousands of glaring white crosses in dozens of our National Cemeteries are reminder enough.

I'm concerned for my country, and I'm not too keen on the entrapments of the politically correct philosophies that stifle American individualism and cripple the economy. Yet, I am utterly confident that if any foreign influence ever miscalculated American dissent for disloyalty and tried to take aggressive advantage of our own in-house bickering, well, as always, the U.S. Marine Corps will be first in, first to die, but they *will* kick ass, pretty or not.

(Grandpa Longbottom joined us for the interview)

Davis readily confessed, "I'll admit being a spoiled brat in my younger days, and my parents weren't too thrilled when I totaled three of their cars during my teenage years, but I knew that after high school I needed to adjust my life. I did my homework and talked to several recruiters, but I soon realized that the toughest challenge would be the Marines."

On June 06, 2005, Davis stepped aboard a Marine bus at Ft. Gillem, GA for Parris Island, SC. "My mom bawled her eyes out," she said. "And I kept asking myself, 'Katherine, what the hell have you done, girl?'"

Davis recalled Parris Island. "Now, there I am, a spoiled brat in basic training at Parris Island for the United States Marines, thinking I'd made a huge mistake. Good Lord, I'd never been screamed at so much in my life, and I didn't see a bed for two days. We were tired, dirty; more unattractive than a four-day old road kill. Shoot; a man wouldn't want to get within ten feet of us. Not that it mattered; a dude was the last thing on our minds, plus the male recruits at Parris Island were even worse. We could smell those guys from a mile away. The training was rough and crude but I wasn't going to quit, I wanted to be a Marine."

Ironically, her most peaceful moments came on the rifle range. She recalled, "Nobody messed with you there, they weren't allowed to. On the rifle range I had time to collect myself." With a fear of heights, the rappel tower on the obstacle course was her biggest challenge. Davis said, "I remember one of the drill instructors; I swear that woman was bipolar; and she kept shouting at me, 'Davis, you're going to hit the ground, you're not going to make a Marine!' but I made it, and finished my 13 weeks of basic."

After her combat training at Camp Lejeune, Davis reported to Ft. Leonard Wood, MO. to learn the ins and outs of the seven ton truck, a Humvee, and a dragon-looking hydraulic beast called the LVS. "I know it's hard to believe," she said. "I totaled three of my parents' automobiles in high school but the Marines trusted me to drive their most expensive equipment. It's called responsibility; and I was finally ready for it." Her first duty assignment was Camp Pendleton, CA where she joined Combat Logistics Battalion 15 and received orders for her first 'float' (sea duty).

She recalled, "I was assigned duty on the assault carrier USS Boxer. We were escorted by two other ships. We're called a MEU, Marine

Expeditionary Unit. We're at the President's beck and call. We go where needed."

Ports-of-call like Hawaii, Singapore, and Australia were preludes to Kuwait and a war called Iraq. "We anchored off Kuwait and took hovercrafts onto the beach where we formed a truck convoy. I cried my last tear on the drive into Iraq, fully understanding I might never see my mom again. But I'm a Marine; I had a job to do." They drove for 21 straight hours in 20 trucks, doing whatever they could to stay awake. Destination: Camp Korean Village in Anbar Province.

For over two months Davis transported needed supplies into the Iraqi city of Rutbah, a 40 minute drive amid IEDs (improvised explosive devices). "It was frightening," she said. "We made 'long' security halts, meaning we got out and looked. A 'short' security check meant we stayed inside the truck doing a '5 and 25', that's looking five meters front and rear, then 25 meters to the sides."

The driver is the 'vehicle commander' regardless of rank. On one 'short' security check Davis spotted white and blue wires sticking out from a guard rail post. "The white wire was clean, no dust or sand on it. We were in trouble." Davis tried to communicate with the convoy via radio, but could not get through. "We were parked right next to an IED and couldn't warn our convoy, it was maddening. I asked the staff sergeant sitting next to me what to do. He said, 'You're the vehicle commander, it's your call.' Well, okay then. If it was a remote control IED the enemy would detonate it when the truck started to move, but if a pressure plate IED was beneath us it would certainly detonate, too. So I decided we'd move with the convoy. Thank God, nothing happened."

They called in the IEDs coordinates; a demolition team checked it; and indeed the device was remote controlled. Davis said, "A Humvee may have unknowingly jammed the IED, or perhaps the trigger-man was too far off." Davis leaned over to whisper in a soft voice so her grandfather couldn't hear. "I hope I'm not being too vulgar, but in a situation like that certain parts of your body puckers big time!" As Katherine scooted back in the chair, Grandpa Longbottom stated, "I didn't hear what you said." Davis replied, "Don't worry about it, Grandpa."

Davis also served five months at Camp Wallied on the Syrian border. As the only female in camp, she was unconcerned about proper conduct from her male counterparts. "The guys were very protective and conducted themselves like gentlemen. Yeah, I got few catcalls from the boys, I mean, a Marine is a Marine and a dude is a dude, but I'm a lady Marine, and we were trained to remain so."

Davis requested one incident be reported above all others. "I'll remember this until the day I die," she said. "We were walking perimeter on security detail in Rutbah guarding our commanding officer as he conducted political business. A little girl ran up and kept staring at me. My neck gator was pulled up (a cloth the lady Marines use to cover their faces because Iraqi men do not want Iraqi women to see other women in positions of power) but I pulled it down and smiled at her. She didn't speak a lick of English but her face lit up like a Christmas tree; she grabbed my blouse and didn't let go for two hours."

"When we began our pull-out she suddenly ran back into a refugee building then returned a minute later. Someone had taught her three words in English. When I leaned over, she said, 'I love you'. Lord, my heart broke into a hundred pieces. I told her, 'I love you, too,' then we were gone. That sweet little girl made my four years of duty and training and war worth the price."

Several Marines from Davis' unit received traumatic brain injuries during combat in Fallujah but fortunately her unit suffered no fatalities. She returned to Camp Pendleton, sailed on one more 'float' aboard the USS Pearl Harbor, and ended her service at Camp Pendleton advising new Marines under deployment.

Recently interviewed for a position in an attorney's office, the interviewer advised Davis that the law firm held their employees to a higher standard. Davis replied, "Ma'am, I'm a United States Marine. I'm already there."

Lou Eisenbrandt
One Vietnam Nurse, Mending And Remembering

Lou Eisenbrandt in Nam

Lou Eisenbrandt was diagnosed with Parkinson's disease 14 years ago, the result of exposure to Agent Orange. Female Angels of Mercy came in contact with the lethal herbicide when cutting away the uniforms on wounded soldiers. I was privileged to meet Lou and listen to her awe-inspiring presentation during the July gathering of the Atlanta Vietnam Veterans Business Association. And this is her story.

From her own words during the presentation: "I have Parkinson's from exposure to Agent Orange, so I've instructed my body to remain still. If I do a Michael J. Fox, please forgive me but I can't help it. I'm also not using a laser pointer because the laser would be all over the place.

"My experiences are no different than other nurses who served in Nam. Ten thousand women served, 7,000 were nurses. I grew up in the small town of Mascoutah, IL, population 3,000. I was the oldest of five, born with a wanderlust in my heart because I knew something else was out there for me.

"I was in nurses training when I stumbled onto an Army program which allowed a nurse to join up, study for three years, then serve for two years. I didn't join for a noble cause or thinking I could change the world, I just wanted to see some of the world, like Germany, Japan, or England. My first port-of-call was officer's training at Ft. Sam Houston, TX in June of 1968. Then I received orders for Ft. Dix, NJ. I packed up my brand new Rambler American and headed for The Garden State.

"I spent nine months at Ft. Dix which was a good thing for me. Some nurses were sent straight from nursing school to Vietnam. Ft. Dix was interesting to say the least. They even had a stockade section and one of my duties was checking daily for improvised weapons. One prisoner escaped, but not on my shift. I usually cared for the soldiers with upper respiratory infections, at one point over 300 soldiers. We also had the fatties and skinnies. If too fat, we put them on diets; if too skinny, they got milk shakes. Oddly, they put these guys in the same ward. The skinnies stayed skinny because the fatties drank all the milk shakes. Before the end of my first year at Ft Dix, I received a manila envelope; 'Congratulations, you're going to Vietnam.' Not the type of see-the-world travel I expected.

"I arrived in Vietnam on November 1, 1969. I had a choice of bases so I picked the 91st Evac at Chu Lai because an old roommate was assigned there. Chu Lai was beautiful, on a hill near a cliff, overlooking the South China Sea. I arrived during Monsoon season, everything was wet; my hooch had double beds, a foot locker, and one fan. Thank goodness my room was in front of the bunker. Chu Lai is located in the skinny part of Vietnam, ocean on one side, mountains in the background.

"I liked flying on choppers since I was an avid photographer. The region is great for photos but I never took any photos of casualties. Chopper pilots are, well, different. They were party animals, loved to party. I spent my first three months in a medical ward treating non-combat related problems, things like hepatitis, malaria, even jungle rot. By the way, the Officer's Club was built on the edge of a cliff. If I recall correctly, we consumed a lot of alcohol in that place.

"Within three months, the chief nurse asked if I wanted the challenge of an emergency room. I accepted her challenge. After we cared for casualties we washed the blood down a drain in the concrete floor with a hose. Head injuries from rotor blades were the worse cases, horrible wounds. If a soldier was not ambulatory we utilized a gurney and used screens to block off the KIAs or DOAs. During triage if we determined a soldier wasn't going to make it he was placed behind a screen then a nurse held his hand and talked to him until he died.

"One time after their village was hit, 99 Vietnamese civilians arrived for care. We treated all of them within 24 hours. When wounded Vietnamese came in, so did the whole family. We also had Vietnamese nurses. They really helped due to culture differences.

"We waterskied but with parameters, like never going out after 1:00pm because that was when sharks arrived. We used a jeep to pull the boat but I have no idea where the jeep, boat, and skis came from. There were local fishermen in LRBs, Little Round Boats, who would wave at us until we threw them a tow rope and pulled them along. They loved it.

"I was 22 years old, young and adventurous. We'd jump in a jeep and travel the heavily mined Highway 1 to visit orphanages or Hue. We took M-16s and helmets, but never encountered problems. They instructed us to not purchase cokes or beer from roadside stands because the VC would booby-trap cans with live grenades. Pull the tab…and, boom!

"Saigon was a trip, pardon the pun. It was crazy. Traffic would go on a red light, then keep on going on a green light. Once a bike ran over my toes; I was standing on the dang sidewalk. Rocket attacks were common at Chi Lai because of all the fuel storage tanks. You know, back then ladies used pink rollers. We couldn't wear helmets during rocket attacks if we had our hair in rollers; it hurt like heck!

"The realities of war? You try to forget them but you never do. Every soldier brought into the emergency room had to have his fatigues cut from his body, fatigues frequently covered with Agent Orange. I recall the missing limbs, arms and legs dangling on shredded flesh, and one soldier we rolled over to check for exit wounds ....his back stayed on the litter. We put him back down. He made it through surgery and we got him to Japan. Don't know if he made it or not. I think of that kid every day.

"You tried to be detached from the suffering, but I had an attachment to a young Lieutenant who came in with his men. His unit took heavy casualties and he wanted to be with them, to see them through their ordeal. Next time it was him, peppered full of shrapnel. We were told he would lose both legs. That's one of the few times I had to walk out of the emergency room. It rattled me. We saved his legs but I've seen him since returning home. His legs are not of much use; he's another boy I think about every day.

"A photo taken of me on my last day in Vietnam shows a young nurse who aged in just one year. You are grateful to be leaving in one piece, but the bond was so strong with the people you worked with that you are also sad about leaving. I was the only female on the flight home. I will never forget my year in Vietnam, it is always with me ... always."

Lou Eisenbrandt returned home then spent six weeks on the road with another nurse, visiting other veteran nurses, doing their best to forget and move on with their lives. Both ladies settled into nursing positions at

Fitzsimmons Army Hospital in Denver. Lou met and married a young attorney named Jim. They've been together for 44 years, have two grown children and two precious grandchildren, and as Lou affectionately stated, 'one big dog.' Her book, "Vietnam Nurse, Mending and Remembering," distributed by Deeds Publishing, is selling like hot cakes.

God bless the Angels of Mercy.

Major Patty Justice
A Purple Heart For Mama Bear

Fob Shank— Home for Mama Bear

August 7, 2013: Forward Operating Base (FOB) Shank, Logar Province in Afghanistan. She remembers a 'thump' followed by the sensation of a big hand picking up her body and squeezing the breath from her lungs. Hurled through the air, her body slams against a blast wall, called an Alaska Wall by the U.S. Military. A water truck packed with 3,000 lbs. of explosives had just detonated 'inside the wire.' Major Patty "Mama Bear" Justice lay wounded and motionless, another casualty of another suicidal terrorist attack. She is 49 years old.

During WWII her father worked on the secretive Manhattan Project to help develop the atomic bomb that ended the war. By the time Patty was born, her father was vice-president of a steel company in Mexico City. She recalled, "When we moved back to the States, I was eight years old, bilingual and with dual-citizenship. I didn't lose dual-citizenship until I took the oath as an officer in the U.S. military."

After high school, Patty attended the New Mexico Military Institute with high hopes of an Army military career upon graduation. An incident in advanced boot camp spoiled the dream. "I ruined my knee," she said. "That terminated my ROTC scholarship so I transferred to Mount Saint Mary's, an all-girl Catholic school in California. After graduation I later worked in defense contracting until moving to Peachtree City, GA in 1989. I met a great guy, we got hitched, and I decided on a career in nursing. First I attended Gordon College before receiving my nursing degree from Brenau University. I worked at Piedmont Hospital for 11 years, until the Twin Towers fell."

Patty received a card in the mail explaining a need for qualified nurses in the military. She said, "I thought, 'shoot, I'll try again,' and I took a chance on being accepted." At 40 years of age, Patty Justice received a direct commission into the US Army. "I didn't even have to wear the butter bars of a 2nd Lt.," she said, grinning. "I was commissioned as a 1st Lieutenant."

After attending an officer basic course at Fort Sam Houston, Texas, Patty was assigned to the 3297th USAH (United States Army Hospital) out of Fort Gordon, Georgia. The battalion moved to Brooke Army Medical Center in San Antonio as the campaign in Iraq heated up. Patty said, "I was there for 18 months. We were the last in a chain of care spectrums. Casualties were flown from Landstuhl Regional Medical Center in Germany into Brooke for the completion of their treatment. Then they went home, or at least to a VA hospital nearest their hometown." During this time the 3297th was disbanded to become the 3274th then reorganized a second time as the 75th Combat Support Hospital out of Tuscaloosa.

Patty returned to Piedmont Hospital after completing her assignment at Brooke. She recalled, "Boy, talk about going back to slow motion. It was like being demoted from the big leagues back to the little league. Piedmont is a great hospital, but a military hospital moves at a more industrious tempo. They expect more." To expand her knowledge as an officer, Patty joined a civil affairs outfit in Dallas, Texas for two years. "Those two years gave me a better rounded background and bestowed really great training," she said. Patty would utilize all the training she ever had for her future deployment.

Up for a promotion to Major without slots available, she received a call from the 228th Combat Support Hospital in San Antonio. Their offer was unembellished: promotion to Major if she'd accept deployment to the 628th Forward Surgical Team hunkered down at an isolated location in Afghanistan called FOB (Forward Operating Base) Shank, nicknamed 'Rocket City' by the troops stationed there. Patty accepted the promotion, and the challenge. Soon nicknamed "Mama Bear" by her colleagues, Major Patty Justice was going to war. From September of 2012 to September of 2013 she would reside with and patch up the troops at 'Rocket City.'

FOB Shank, Afghanistan: "Well, it reminded me of the movie MASH; we lived in tents, no real roads, just about everything brought in by air, and that included the wounded and dying. We stayed busy and learned a lot about different cultures, the Afghans and Nepalese. Afghan men in the villages could not understand a woman in uniform, packing a .45 automatic, and so bold as to look them in the eye. They just couldn't comprehend that."

Mama Bear kept count of the action. She recalled, "We got hit 278 times during my tour, mainly in the mornings then into the afternoons, but not very often at night. Even though we were 'blacked-out' at night, I had the impression many of the enemy fighters were basically lazy, like, 'It's time for bed, see you in the morning.' Our south side base did get hit at night so I guess it depended on which area had the laziest fighters. Anyway, we received mortars, RPGs, and sniper fire on a regular basis."

Her comments on the base medical field facility: "They did a great job considering we only had 14 people. We were on call 24/7, no shift work because the shifts depended on casualties. A 72 hour shift was nothing for us, yet the next time we'd only work four hours. We saw and treated a minimum of 1,100 patients. These were not minor injuries. We dealt with the results of IEDs and combat, severed limbs; people absolutely blown away. During the fall and winter we mainly took care of Afghan soldiers, except for the American soldiers hit by sniper fire or suffering from frost bite or hypothermia. It was horribly cold during the winter. But then the 'killing season' began, May through December, and the American casualties really picked up."

When discussing American soldiers, she stated, "Those guys are good, resilient, and do what they are told. The average age of a soldier was about 20, our field surgical team about 25, and there I am a 49 year old Mama Bear fussin' over our boys."

August 7, 2013 — "Our small medical facility and living quarters were no more than a 30 second walk from 'the wire'. We lived close to where we worked because we had to respond quickly for the medevac flights, coming in and going out. That night we were hit by mortars and had to attend an after action meeting in the morning. I forgot something and had to return to the tent which put me outside the protective wall. Suddenly, 'Boom', and that's all I remembered."

The 'boom' was a water truck. The truck was stolen a couple of months prior to the explosion, the two truck drivers found beheaded. During the interim, insurgents jam-packed the truck with 3,000 lbs. of military explosives, slipped through an Afghan checkpoint two months later, then detonated the truck and themselves. The explosion created a 75 foot gap in the protective wire.

Momma Bear regained consciousness 45 minutes later, strapped to a stretcher, dazed and in pain. She recalled, "The base was home to an American Mountain Division, Rangers, and special forces guys. Some of the men had just returned from night combat duties and were sacked out when the truck exploded. Those guys didn't hesitate. They grabbed their weapons and gear and hit the perimeter in their underwear to ward off any ground attack. Luckily, there wasn't a ground attack."

The explosion and resulting injuries dislocated Mama Bear's shoulder and hip. Her ears resonated with a thousand church bells and continued to resonate for weeks to come. Plus, as later discovered, she received a moderate TBI (traumatic brain injury). Flown via medevac chopper to Bagram Air Base along with a trauma surgeon suffering from shrapnel wounds, Mama Bear's next port-of-call for proper recovery should have been Landstuhl Regional Medical Center in Germany.

"No way," she said. "After a few days I told them I was just fine, my fingers and toes worked okay, my trigger finger still functioned, and I was ready to go back to FOB Shank." When they asked about the terrible ringing in her ears, she replied, "No ringing whatsoever." Mama Bear was lying through her Mama Bear teeth, but the fib worked. She returned to Rocket City to work alongside her colleagues and completed her tour. One month later, Momma Bear rotated home with her unit.

More than qualified, combat veteran nurse Patty Justice found quick employment at the Atlanta Medical Center Trauma Unit. She also needed additional corrective surgery on her shoulder.

Now the fog of military paper-shuffling reared its ludicrous head when Patty received several emails from Bagram Air Base inquiring about her Purple Heart. She never received a Purple Heart and always wondered why, so Patty contacted the deputy chief nursing officer she served with in Afghanistan. Patty said, "He was fit to be tied when he heard about the screw-up." Through his and Patty's persistence the truth was finally exposed. The unprocessed paperwork for seventeen individual Purple Heart recipients had been discovered inside a desk drawer at Bagram Air Base, including Patty's. She stated, "Shoot, I was thinking about going to Fort Benning to purchase my own Purple Heart!"

No, that's not the way it happened and she didn't have to purchase a Purple Heart at Fort Benning. In a very special ceremony, Major Patty C. Justice was presented her Purple Heart on Friday, December 5, 2014 at the Walk of Heroes War Memorial at Black Shoals Park in Rockdale County, Georgia by the Georgia Department, Military Order of the Purple Heart & Chapter 465.

Well done, Mama Bear, well done.

Peter Elizabeth Wolfe – Tsalagi (Cherokee)
A Policeman And Patriot Called Peter

Peter Elizabeth Wolfe — Cherokee Native American

The first thing noticeable as I entered the interview room was the rifle clenched in the hands of the interviewee. I recognized the weapon as the mainstay of the WWII Japanese soldier: an Arisaka 7.7mm Type 99 infantry rifle. An interviewee armed with a rifle would normally cause me a flash of trepidation, but the interviewee, Peter, was a cop.

Peter was also the first woman I've met with my own first name, Peter, derived via Latin 'Petra', from the Greek word 'Petros', meaning 'stone' or 'rock'. Jesus gave Simon the name 'Kaphan' or 'Cephas' denoting 'stone' in Aramaic, thus his name, Simon Peter. Peter Elizabeth Wolfe is the epitome of a 'rock', both in terms of a patriot and an individual who has devoted her life to the service of others. And this is her story.

Peter was raised in the customs of the Tsalagi Native American Indians, more commonly called the Cherokees of North Carolina. Her dad, Earl Wolfe, served in the Pacific during WWII with the 136th Infantry as an ambulance and truck driver. The 136th battled in New Guinea,

Luzon, and fought virtually alone for 20 straight days against fanatic Japanese on the island of Morotai. Thus, his ownership of the Type 99 rifle.

Peter stated, "My father never told me the whole story, but he made it clear that either the Jap soldier or he would be taking a rifle home as a souvenir. Since dad preferred the latter, he did what he had to do."

Her parents' first son, Peter Allen, died at the age of 3 months. Part of his spirit needed to pass to the next child, ironically a female, thus the name Peter Elizabeth Wolfe. Peter was born in Chattanooga where her father served as a police officer. During the summers, the family spent time in Florence, SC harvesting crops of cotton and tobacco. Peter also spent time with her grandparents on the Tahlequah Indian reservation in Oklahoma.

Peter commented on reservation life: "Tahlequah is also the Cherokee National Capital, but the people were sad, their spirit was broken, they didn't want to be there. You could see it in their eyes, a sadness deep in their souls." Nevertheless patriotic, her mother's brother and all the males from her dad's family served in the military. One uncle served on the ill-fated USS Indianapolis. Torpedoed on July 30, 1945, 300 sailors went down with the ship, 900 sailors went into the water; after sharks finished their feast only 316 men were rescued. Peter's uncle had been transferred off the Indianapolis a couple of days before her final cruise.

As Peter matured, she told her father a career in law enforcement was in her future. Her father, familiar with the 'mean streets', emphatically stated, "No!" He did agree to a military career. While attending college at the University of Tennessee at Chattanooga, Peter became the first female to sign up for the ROTC program. She recalled, "I had to wear a male cadet's uniform, pass a male physical training test, and live with a lot of animosity from the 'all-Boys' Club. But I earned my butter bars."

Commissioned as a 2nd Lieutenant in the reserves, Peter Elizabeth spent the next 27 years in the reserves and active reserves. Her specialties in the military: expertise as transportation movement officer and logistics expert, and platoon leader of training and maintenance with ¼ ton, 2.5 ton, 5 ton trucks, and the monstrous 10 ton Dragon Wagon tank hauler. Her experience would be exceedingly needed as the American military geared up for the Gulf War.

She recalled, "We had to move the entire military to the Persian Gulf; it was like the military was saying, 'Uh, how do we do this?' The 82nd and advanced combat-ready elements were deployed into holding positions to block Saddam Hussein's next foray, but reserve units faced an almost impossible task gearing up for a major war. The lack of preparation was unbelievable."

Now a Captain, Peter was assigned to the 2nd Army as a transportation movement officer at Fort Gillem. "You don't grab an M-16 and just go marching off to war," she recalled. "The water purification units were all in the reserves so we had to gear up that entity. Units had outdated weapons and equipment, some didn't have enough, so we merged the units. Then the cat fights started between unit commanders. We felt like we were in the 'Oh, crap' mode."

Peter worked 16 to 18 hours a day, slept under her desk, argued with state governors over their reserve units, calmed down shell-shocked administrative supervisors, and deciphered inaccurate 'status' reports.

"That was just the beginning," she said. "Think about the problems of personnel, doctors concerned about their practices and patients, men and women worried about their mortgages or leases, what to do with the kids, what about power of attorney. We had to call in JAG people, update wills and insurance policies, divorced people had obsolete info in their files ... even the Pentagon, or as we called it, 'the Puzzle Palace', was shocked by the lack of coordination." Pausing for a moment, she then observed, "Let's put it this way, it was like a herd of turtles racing across a field of peanut butter."

Once the shooting started, Peter and the 2nd had to plan for the return of forces once the shooting stopped. The 2nd also helped plan the huge Heroes Parade in Washington, DC. Her later assignments included the Pentagon, Bad Kreuznach in Germany with 3rd Army, command position at Sunny Point, NC, and her most vivid memory of service in Bosnia, "I was in Bosnia for two months before I saw a complete kid with all the fingers and toes, arms and legs. Land mines took a horrible toll on the children."

Major Peter Elizabeth Wolfe retired from the Army Reserves the same day she graduated as a Rockdale County Deputy Sheriff. She said, "My lifelong dream was law enforcement. I've been doing what I love to do for almost 16 years." Well-known and respected in the community, she is a 'rock' in personality and policing.

Peter lost her husband, Lt. Col. Robert Timian of the 82nd Airborne, in January of 2012 of complications from exposure to Agent Orange. Lt. Col. Timian served three tours in Vietnam. Herself a cancer survivor, Peter continues to serve the citizens of Rockdale County as a fifth generation law enforcement officer from the proud Tsalagi Tribe of North Carolina.

Mary Babnik Brown
Bombardiers Prefer Blondes

The musical comedy, *Gentlemen Prefer Blondes,* released in 1953, starred two of Hollywood's most gorgeous bombshells, Marilyn Monroe and Jane Russell. Marilyn Monroe, a blonde throughout her movie career, was paid $500.00 a week due to contract obligations. Russell, a natural brunette, better known and more experienced, received $200,000.00 for the film. So, is it the brunettes who really have more fun? Just sayin'.

I jest. However, had WWII American bombardiers known their

secretive Norden bombsight's crosshairs were made from hair donated by American blondes, they also would have preferred a fine looking blonde-haired lady. It all started with the failure of black widow spider webbing.

Not going into great detail concerning the Norden bombsight, but suffice to say it was developed pre-WWII in secrecy and remained top secret throughout the war. Great efforts were initiated to keep the bombsight from falling into enemy hands, like surrounding the bombsight with booby-trapped explosives to be detonated by crewmembers if the devise was in danger of being seized by an adversary. Legend has it that the bombsight was so accurate, a bomb dropped from 20,000 feet could find the entrance to a pickle barrel. Uh, 'legend' also means myths or fairytales. The Norden bombsight was good, but not quite as precise as alleged.

The Army Air Force had experimented with several types of materials for the crosshairs on the Norden bombsight, which included the use of black widow spider webbing. The webbing was tough and practical under certain low level conditions, but at higher altitudes, like 20,000 feet, the spider webbing could not withstand the disparities in temperatures, especially below freezing. It was discovered, however, (history does not record by whom the discovery was made) that fine human blonde hair was perfect for the job, as long as the hair had not been treated with chemicals or heat (curling iron). Pure, fine, human blonde hair resisted climatic changes and below freezing temperatures. In short, natural blondes with pristine hair were suddenly in big demand for the bombsight, meteorological contraptions, and other scientific paraphernalia to make precise measurements of humidity that is critical in the production of military aircraft and numerous war related materials.

The War Department had access to an ample supply of blonde hair from European women. Why European women? Ya got me, I have no idea. But as war engulfed Europe and the blonde hair source was cut off (no pun intended), the War Department shifted attention to American blondes, especially regions with large Scandinavian populaces, like the Dakotas and Minnesota. So, how does one recruit blondes to contribute cuttings of their locks to support an ultra-top secret program without breaking security? Easy. You advertise in the newspapers.

Of course the newspaper ads were vague concerning the need for blonde hair, only noting the donation was to assist the war effort. The New York Times reported in March of 1943, an 11-year old girl from Sea Cliff, Long Island, Anita Hochberg, sent 14" of her 'patriotic blonde hair' to be used as needed. Doris Jahncke, a 16-year-old from Durbin, N.D, sent a cutting of her hair, tied with a red, white, and blue ribbon, to be tested. The Army accepted the offer, then Doris sent 30" of her tresses to Washington, DC. Countless American women contributed their blonde locks to help gain the victory.

The best known and most recognized contributor was a woman from Pueblo, Colorado, named Mary Babnik Brown. A child of Slovenia immigrants and the oldest of seven siblings, her father abandoned the family in 1920. Twelve year old Mary (actually Mitzi, a Slovenian name, but she Americanized it to Mary) quit school when she was 12 years old to help support her mother, a domestic helper, and help support the family. Her first job was as a domestic: $5.00 per week. Her siblings also helped to keep food on the table by picking up chunks of coal on railroad tracks that had fallen from coal cars. At 13, Mary lied about her age and found a full-time job at the National Broom Factory for 75 cents a day. That was her starting salary; Mary stayed with the company for 42 years.

She enjoyed dancing and became well-known in Pueblo. Mary picked up her dancing hobby in her early teens and won many dance contests. Her favorite ballroom was the Arcadia, where she became known as 'Arcadia Mary.' She taught GIs how to dance during the war, and was quoted as saying, "My first love is family, but dancing is my second."

The blonde hair ad stated they only wanted hair which had not been treated with chemicals, or a hot iron, plus needed to be at least 22" long. Mary had no problem qualifying. Her hair had never been cut, was 34" long and stretched down to her knees. She washed it with 'pure soap' twice a week, combed it twice a day, and never used a curling iron. Her long blonde hair was a source of pride for Mary. Usually wrapped around her head in a braid, she picked up the nickname "lady with the crown."

Believing a donation of her locks patriotic, Mary sent samples to the Washington Institute of Technology where it was tested, analyzed, and found to be perfect for crosshairs. Advised of the test results, Mary cut off her hair and sent her locks to support the war effort. She cried for two weeks.

Mary Babnik married a man named Carl Brown near the end of the war, becoming Mary "Mitzi" Babnik Brown. Moss did not grow under Mary's feet. She became the first woman to hold the position as vice-president of the State Federation of Labor plus joined and became an active member of the Democratic Party. Mary also served as vice-president, then president of the Slovenian National Benefit Society. She was never informed as to what her hair had been used for during the war nor did she ask. That is, until a letter arrived from Washington DC dated November 6, 1987. It read as follows:

Dear Mrs. Brown:

I was pleased to learn of your strong love for our nation, of how you donated your hair to the war effort during WWII and its use as crosshairs in the Norden bombsight, helping our bombardier's sight enemy ground targets in Europe and the Pacific. You can be very proud of a selfless act that set a splendid example during wartime.

When I hear of such patriotism, I am reminded of what an honor it is to be called to serve as President of the United States.

Nancy joins me in sending our warm best wishes for a very Happy 80th Birthday.

Sincerely, Ronald Reagan.

On November 17, 1990, Mary received a special achievement awarded from the Colorado Aviation Society in a ceremony at the U.S. Air Force Academy in Colorado Springs, CO. She was also inducted into their Hall of Fame.

Remember Paul Harvey, the famous radio personality and his nationally broadcast program *The Rest of the Story*? He told Mary's story to the nation on November 19, 1990.

On November 22, 1991, Pueblo, Colorado declared the 22nd of November as "Mary Babnik Brown Day." The ceremony was recorded by NBC-TV and aired on NBC's *The Story Behind the Story*.

Mary's hair was even mentioned in a wartime telegram sent by the Enola Gay's (B-29 bomber that dropped the atomic bomb on Hiroshima in WWII) bombardier, Thomas Ferebee. Stone Mountain resident Theodore "Dutch" Van Kirk was Enola Gay's navigator.

Now enters the proverbial fog of war. Half-truths, deceptions, misinformation, 'classified information' never classified since the information never existed and/or a feint to hoodwink an adversary.

Did the War Department and the U.S. Army request blonde hair during WWII? Yes, officially documented, mainly for use in the meteorological instruments.

Was it used for crosshairs in the Norden bombsight? Doubtful, no concrete evidence exists, yet rumors and stories still prevail. The few Norden bombsights still in existence have crosshairs etched into the glass via diamond cutters.

My personal research found no record of a Paul Harvey *'The Rest of the Story'* narrative on Mary Babnik Brown. And NBC, according to their programing history, never produced a show called *The Story Behind the Story*.

Was President Ronald Reagan misled or deceived, or just being a good patriotic American President whose underlings failed to do their research? Is the letter an internet or research engine hoax?

Did Mary "Mitzi" Babnik Brown even exist, and did she really donate her blonde hair to the war effort? Yes, documented, and most of her belated awards are open for public scrutiny.

Believable stories, propaganda, distortions, a little lie here and a little fib there, all products of man's inhumanity to man in the undertaking called war.

Beginning in early 1945, Allied aircraft were suddenly followed by unexplained lights and fireballs. The name given to the odd phenomena was Foo-Fighters. Since 1948, however, they have been identified as *flying saucers*.

"*Sieg Heil, Sieg Heil,*" one of the marches used by the Nazis and Adolf Hitler to rally supporters was a tune taken from Harvard University's "Fight, Fight, Fight" song. True or false? True.

My skepticism on 'shaky ground' stories had its genesis at the Intelligence School in Denver, Colorado. The first thing taught us was, "Don't believe anything you hear, and only half of what you see." Good advice.

Ruth Jones
Struggle, Sacrifice, And Salvation

The Robin's egg blue Magnolia Assisted Living Home is nestled between a Thai Restaurant and Hispanic taxicab parking lot about one mile from my front door, so my trek for the interview was negligible.

I'd interviewed a few veterans living at Magnolia but this was my first WWII Home Front candidate from the facility. Her two loving sons, Donald and James, joined our discussion since 'Mom' had recently developed a bit of a problem with facts and timelines. That tends to happen when one survives beyond the Golden Years to the memory-filled age of 97.

Frail, in failing health, yet deeply religious, Ruth Jones gave all the appearances of a bubbly, humorous individual tempered by hardships that fine-tuned the personality of a survivor. One theme continuous repeated during the interview was Ruth's good-natured approach to life in general.

"No need to grumble," she said more than a couple of times. "Life's not a bed of roses, rather a constant sidestep to avoid the fertilizer."

As she recalled the years, I realized this gracious Southern Belle of yesteryear was a history book of knowledge. *What a shame*, I thought, that elderly citizens such as Ruth are restricted to a small room and consider 'a trip' toddling or pushing a walker to the front dining room.

Here's a thought: Instead of inviting a politician or community leader with selfish motives to local schools for a presentation, invite a senior citizen to speak to the students concerning the real facts of life without the 'spin' of manipulation. If the senior can't travel, the students can, and a field trip to an assisted living facility would give them an insight into this thing we call 'life' that will serve the students far better than a field trip to Six Flags Amusement Park.

The Greatest Generation is leaving us at an accelerated rate. Our country does not need to bury their history with them.

Me And Mrs. Jones

In 1823 Georgian George Merritt built a corn mill south of Hightower

Trail called Costley's Mill. Native American Creek and Cherokee Indians in the Rockdale County prefecture helped rebuild the mill several times after devastating fires but when General Sherman passed directly in front of the mill during his "March to the Sea" and threatened to torch the mill again, Winnie Puckett grabbed a pistol and stood her ground. "You take one more step," Winnie threatened the startled general, "And I'll blow your damn head off!" Apparently Sherman realized Winnie wasn't bluffing and swiftly backed down. He and Winnie talked; Sherman eventually promised not to burn down the mill, then Winnie offered the general a big plug of chewing tobacco as a peace offering. Rockdale County history does not record if Sherman accepted the plug or not.

"Winnie Puckett was my aunt," Magnolia Assisted Living resident Ruth Jones said. "She didn't put up with nothing from nobody, and that included Sherman."

Born in 1915 in a dwelling behind Honey Creek Baptist Church, Ruth said, "One of my aunts played the piano there. I'd sit beside her, but didn't want to. I wanted to go outside and play with the other kids."

At the age of 15, Ruth lost her mother in a car accident. "I never had a permanent home after that," she said. "I was sort of passed around to different relatives." At the age of 19, Ruth received a proposal of marriage from Frank Jesse Jones. He promised Ruth, "When I get enough money to buy you a coat, we're getting married."

Orphaned as a teenager, a survivor of the Great Depression, Ruth's faith helped her in the struggle to feed two boys and two nephews, plus meet a multitude of financial obligations when Frank and her younger brother, Norman Rice, joined millions of men and women defending our country in WWII.

"I worked part time as a waitress, an employee of the Crown Candy Company and A&P Bakery," Ruth recalled. "Sugar was rationed back then so the companies never had enough sugar to create full time work.

Everything went to the war effort." Asked if she missed nylons, Ruth said, "Nylons? We were lucky to have socks!"

Even as she struggled to put food on the table, Ruth lived with the constant fear of receiving the hated Postal Telegraph from the War Department. "We all lived with that gut-wrenching fear," she said.

Her younger brother, Norman, enlisted in the Navy in June of '42 at the age of 18, trained at Norfolk, VA then studied to be an Aviation Radioman in Bedford Springs, PA and Millington, TN. He graduated from Millington in Feb of '43, sailed from San Diego the next month, and on April 30 Ruth received the telegram that Norman was missing in action.

"We don't know much about it," she said. "The War Department only told us he was in a plane searching for downed airmen. They don't know if they were shot down or had a mechanical problem, but the bodies were never recovered." Her voice softened to a whisper. "He was just a baby, a sweet boy, and he loved the Navy. Going to war was his first time out of Georgia. Norman always used the word 'swell' to describe his newfound world."

Her son, Donald, recalled, "I was 10 or 11 and walking home from school. A lot of the neighborhood kids were outside our house, and when I walked up they said, 'Your Mom's brother has been killed.' When I went inside, Mom was standing in front of our front window, bawling her eyes out."

Her youngest son, James, recalled, "I was only about five when it happened. I asked Mom what was wrong, but she'd just say, 'nothing' and continue with her private grief."

Ruth had written and mailed a letter to Norman on April 20, the date of his death. The Post Office returned the letter on May 1st with the notation 'Return to Sender' and a 'reason block' marked 'Unclaimed'. Ruth received a payment voucher for Norman's life, $842.40 in insurance money by monthly payments of $15.60. Norman's personal effects were never returned.

Her husband, Frank, was destined for a place in history. Drafted into the Army, he never discussed his obligations with Ruth understanding the heartache she carried for her brother and not wanting Ruth to excessively worry about him.

What is known of her husband's service culminates with the surrender of Japan. Frank Jesse Jones boarded the troopship *General W. A. Mann* after the war and by Nov, '45 was part of the occupation forces stationed in the city of Nagasaki, the second city to experience an atomic bomb. Frank's health suffered as a result. Ruth and Frank finally reunited in 1946.

"I remember Frank arriving on the train at Fort Mac," she said. "When I saw him step off the train I jumped out of the car and ran as fast as I could to greet him. Everyone there was running for their loved ones. Our war was finally over."

Frank and Ruth were married for sixty years until his death in 1994. The Honey Creek Baptist Church's cemetery is the final resting place for several of Ruth's relatives, including a commemorative tombstone for her younger brother, Norman. Norman Rice is also etched in granite in front of the Rockdale County Courthouse.

"People call us The Greatest Generation," Ruth said. "We didn't have the time to think about being great; we were too busy making a living and winning a world war."

Wilsonia "Soni" Browne
The Show Must Go On

Wilsonia 'Soni' Brown

Adopted at age five by a couple who owned a nursing home in Mount Vernon, NY, Wilsonia "Soni" Browne loved to sing to and entertain the residents. Before her 12th birthday, the family moved to Miami, Florida.

Soni recalled, "After high school I attended Central State College in Ohio, but I wasn't really ready for college. My mother and I had a few words about me dropping out, so I decided to join the Army. I figure that way people wouldn't tell me what to do all the time."

March, 1967: In basic training at Fort McClellan, Alabama, Soni quickly learned the Army was the wrong outfit for independent thinkers.

"I slipped on my PJs my mother had bought me, but our 1st Sergeant told me I was in the wrong PJs. I replied, 'No, these are the right PJs; my mother bought them for me.' Then she informed me my PJs weren't regulation, so I repeated, 'Yes they are, my mother bought them for me.' Well, I ended up scrubbing three flights of stairs with a toothbrush."

The rifle range: "I'd never shot a gun before in my life," she said. "There I was with a loaded M-16 and scared to death. I pulled the trigger and was startled by the kickback. I just kept pulling the trigger and somehow qualified. Then I had to drive a 2½-ton truck with a straight shift. I never had done that before either, but I sure as heck learned. Later in training we even had to drive a tank. Once again we were scared to death, believing we'd kill each other. But we did okay, and started having fun."

During Soni's third week at Fort McClelland, the 3rd Army Soldier Show arrived on base and put on a performance for the recruits. "I was captivated," Soni recalled. "That's what I wanted to do."

Soni received permission to talk to the base commander. "The Major wanted me to be her personal driver, but I respectfully refused and explained that I wanted to sing. From that day until we graduated from basic, I sang the National Anthem at the weekly graduation ceremonies."

Her next port-of-call after graduating from basic training was Fort McPherson, Georgia, home of the 3rd Army Soldier Show. At her first audition, Soni was asked in typical Army fashion, "Why did they send you here? You certainly don't have a voice."

"I was devastated," Soni recalled. "But I did get to talk to the producer and was told to go back to the barracks. I was on pins and needles for two days awaiting my fate." After the two day wait, she received the good news: acceptance in the Soldier Show. "I was so excited," Soni said. "I packed my bags and moved into their barracks."

With her singing temporarily on hold, Soni learned to care for the Soldier Show's bus and 18-wheel tractor/trailer rig. "I was still in the U.S. Army," she said, grinning. "I enjoyed the group, the camaraderie, and entertaining the soldiers. For me it was very rewarding."

Production themes included the 1960s hits, *'Fiddler on the Roof'* and *'Up, Up, and Away.'* Soni recalled, "We also produced an Asian theme that included me coming down inside a pagoda for my solo. I was very proud of that, and happy to do it for the troops."

Notwithstanding, entertaining troops in time of war can be an emotional experience. The likes of Bob Hope knew that, but the entertainers bit their lower lips and did what they did best: entertaining the troops with a show before, after, and sometimes during combat. Hope's Christmas Special at Long Bien, Vietnam in 1971 was filmed before a jam-packed audience. A year later in 1972, Long Bien was deserted and overgrown with weeds. Of that experience, Bob Hope said, "Well, this is like it is now ... and this is the way it should be. All those happy, smiling, beautiful faces are gone, and most of them are really where they belong, at home with their loved ones." Wilsonia "Soni" Browne saw a lot of those same kind of faces, before they went to war, then after they came home.

In her own words: "We entertained the soldiers going to Vietnam from Fort Benning and Fort Campbell. Many were leaving the next day. We did our best and kept a cheerful tone, but I remember all those young faces just out of high school, just making the best of it. At one show, I recognized a boy that graduated from high school with me. He was crying and I wanted to cry with him, but I couldn't. Even the officers and NCOs looked so young. It was heartbreaking.

"We didn't understand Vietnam. We'd discuss the war on the bus, but we couldn't come to grips with what the war really meant, what it was really all about. Seeing all those young soldiers leaving for Vietnam was an emotional roller coaster ride for us, but entertaining the soldiers after they came home was an emotional nightmare.

"Most of them had been back for a week or two when we put on our show. We noticed the change immediately, the wheelchairs, the bandages, the braces, lost vision, and lost limbs. The soldiers were downcast, like they were afraid to be back in the 'unknown', that 'unknown' being their own country. The nation was divided by the war which made it hard on the returning soldiers, I mean, they had no idea as to how they'd be received by the public. Many of them wanted to stay in the military because it's all they knew, but they were being forced out because of their injuries.

"The injured soldiers were obvious, but the psychologically and mentally broken soldiers weren't. We quickly learned many of them couldn't carry on a conversation, some smiled, others were like statues, no response whatsoever. The 'approachable' ones were pointed out by the officers and NCOs, but we'd be warned about the 'unapproachables.' It was so sad, their lives would never be the same. There were no yellow ribbons for these boys."

Credited with four years of military service, Soni earned a degree in Social Welfare at the University of Maryland and Miami Dade Junior College. She has dedicated her life to helping others, both young and old. Soni worked as a student counselor at Fort Valley State College and Morris Brown University, but her heart belongs to the elderly. She has served as Program Director for numerous assisted-living facilities and has dedicated her skills for the past 15 years to the large Remington House Retirement/Assisted-living facility in Conyers, Georgia.

Her final thoughts: "I remember my first weekend pass in basic training when we were refused service at a local soda fountain because of our race. We heard the ugly statement, 'We don't serve Negroes in here.' Well, our 1st Sergeant and base commander heard about the incident and made sure that never happened again. The base commander told the soda fountain jerks in an unyielding voice, 'These ladies are serving their country, and by God, they'll be served here, too!' They took a stand for us, and I will always remember it was the military that took that stand.

"You know, I think all high school graduates need to serve in the military or in some other capacity for the country for about two years, to learn what freedom really means and to judge people on the content of their character, not on their race, creed, or color, but on the person inside."

Susan Clotfelter Jimison
I Can't Tell You How Long I Cried

Susan Clotfelter Jimison

Susan was the youngest of five siblings. Mark was the only son and the apple of his father's eye. The father had served in the South Pacific during WWII as the radioman and waist gunner on a B-24 Liberator heavy bomber. Their father knew of war. And this is their story, the story of one family and the pain that war leaves in its wake.

Susan Clotfelter Jimison was born east of Los Angeles, CA in the small town of Covina. When she was three years old, the family moved to Hialeah, Florida where Susan spent her teenage years and young adulthood. "I liked Florida in the '60's and '70's," she said. "But not now. Florida is just too commercialized."

Susan was on summer vacation in June of 1969 awaiting the transition as a 14 year old student from 9th grade junior high school to the 10th grade in senior high school. Her brother, Mark, had been 'in-country' in Vietnam since September 25, 1968. "I was still a kid when Mark left for Vietnam in 1968," she recalled. "My father had used the GI Bill after WWII to learn to fly and flew private aircraft. Mark flew with dad and had earned a fixed-wing rating before he enlisted in the Army in 1967. Of course he was drawn into Army aviation and trained at Fort Wolters, Fort Rucker, and Hunter Army Air Field to earn his wings as a chopper pilot flying the Cobra gunship. He didn't care what he flew, he just wanted to be in the air, and he loved what he was doing. I don't recall us being overly concerned for Mark's safety since he was such a good pilot. But dad, being a combat veteran, was worried but kept it to himself. That's the way dad was."

Mark was assigned to the 361st Aviation Company Escort (The Pink Panthers) at Camp Holloway in Pleiku, Vietnam. Normally his escort flying provided cover for clandestine Special Forces missions into Laos and Cambodia. Mark had already been shot down twice, received the Distinguished Flying Cross with two oak leaf clusters, a Bronze Star, the Army Commendation Medal, Air Medal, and many more.

June 16, 1969, however, was another story. Mark, and a rookie flying his first mission named Michael Mahowald, volunteered to fly air support for a resupply convoy moving through a 'hot area' between Dak To and Ben Het. At tree top level, they soon received enemy small arms fire from a concealed bunker. Bullets raked the gunship, the Cobra quickly inverted then crashed on top of the bunker, killing the enemy soldiers. Having gone down in enemy territory, a recovery was impossible.

Susan recalled the day two men in uniform showed up at their front door. "My sister, Redina, was getting married that day. Mark had introduced her to the guy she was marrying. They had worked together at the Miami Airport for Bendix airplane parts. Dad and one of my other sisters answered the door, the two men came in, told my father something, and gave him some paperwork. Dad quickly walked them back to the door and let them out, then turned around and told us, "We're not going to talk about this today."

So my sister got married and after they left for their honeymoon, dad sat us down and broke the news to us. At that point Mark was only missing, but looking back at wedding photos it showed my father's anguish, I mean he was always smiling, but not in those wedding photos. I think dad pretty much knew he had lost his only son. I was young, and thought Mark was just 'missing' and that he would be found. We were concerned, of course, but my father seemed to be holding it together and was being strong, so we thought Mark was just 'missing', it's as simple as that."

Although the family received frequent telegrams advising that 'they' were still looking for Mark, in reality he and Michael had gone down in enemy territory and 'they' couldn't get in there for recovery efforts. It's as simple as that.

Susan continued, "My dad died in 1996 so he never knew this, but later on I got my hands on a copy of my brother's individual deceased personnel file. I contacted the person that went to the crash site and removed the bodies from the aircraft, a man named Glynn Koehler, and he said that he had never received a phone call like mine. I just told him I wanted to thank him for what he did, because I'd met a lot of people over the past 27 years that never did get their loved one home. Mr. Koehler said he remembered the recovery, that he'd done a lot of them for Graves Registration, and said he recalled two unusual things that happened. He said a Major was on the scene who was my brother's commanding officer, who said he felt like he needed to be there, for Mark.

"The next odd thing was that somebody in that aircraft was wearing someone else's clothes and 'they' almost notified the wrong family. My present husband told me the story in 1999 in a big long email that the guy in the front seat of my brother's aircraft was on his first mission, had recently been checked out to fly, but didn't have his own Nomex. (High-tech fire-retardant fibers in clothing worn by people who work jobs with a high risk of fire, like fighter pilots, oil drilling personnel, chopper pilots, ect.) Michael was wearing my husband's Nomax clothes. You see, my husband, who is also named Mike, was scheduled to fly with my brother that day, but the other Mike had been 'in-country' for weeks and had yet to fly a mission, so he talked Mark and my husband into letting him go. Therefore, my husband, Mike, gave, Mike, the replacement front-seater, his Nomax clothing.

"My husband got to Vietnam in May and Mark was killed in June, so they had a very short time together. I had corresponded via email with my present husband about my brother but we didn't meet face to face until 1999 while attending a Vietnam Helicopter Pilots Association reunion in Nashville. We married in 2006."

Once Mark's remains were recovered and a positive ID made, his parents received a telegram stating that Mark had actually been killed in combat in 1969. Susan said, "My parents were members of that older generation, they showed no emotion, nobody talked about it, and we had a private service with only the immediate family present. Dad had what remains were sent back cremated and spread Mark's ashes by himself from his airplane over the Atlantic Ocean right off Miami Beach. My dad was like Frank Sinatra, he did it his way."

When asked her own response to that 'final' telegram, Susan said, "Mark was my only brother...I can't tell you how long I cried. It happened between the 9th and 10th grade, I wasn't in high school yet, and it's still weird. I can still post something on Facebook about Mark and get a response from a classmate who didn't know Mark was killed in Vietnam. I mean, you just don't sit down in homeroom and tell classmates, 'Oh, by the way, my brother was killed in Vietnam.' Some people knew about it, but not many. You just sucked it up and go on, especially when the war was so unpopular at the time."

An enduring heartache: "Mark will always be with me. It was so painful to watch the nightly news in those final years of the Vietnam War. Sometimes I even expect to suddenly see him or thought maybe he was still just 'missing'."

When asked if the heartache ever softened, Susan replied, "Oh, I don't know. He died in 1969, I graduated from high school in 1972, and married for the first time in 1973 ... I guess you just go on when you lose a loved one. One huge episode for me was when the Moving Wall came to Port Everglades. I had never seen Mark's name on a headstone, since his ashes were spread over the ocean, so I felt like he finally had a place on earth that bore his name, and that was important to me. I saw the Moving Wall a few times so by the time I visited the real Wall in Washington, DC I was not as emotional as the first time."

The genesis of her book *Dear Mark:* "My father died suddenly in 1996, just after I had moved out to Washington. I spent that last year with him, but I was devastated, he just didn't wake up one day. It was so unexpected. Then after his death my sister gave me her old computer, shoot, I didn't even know how to use it. I had Mark's pictures, he loved to take pictures, so I had a lot to go on, so I decided to just play around on the computer and within two weeks I found a guy Mark had gone to flight school with. Then I discovered this group online called the Vietnam Helicopter Flight Crew Network, and that guided me to contact with others who served with Mark.

"Then I received an invitation to come to a reunion of his unit. The first one was very emotional, I met a lot of people, and a few of the guys I knew they had to have hung out with Mark because they were in several of his photos. I saw pictures of Mark I'd never seen before, so being able to spend time with these guys gave me an insight as to how Mark lived over there, what he ate, where did he sleep, what did he do for those first nine months in Vietnam. By finding and talking with these guys I got to know my brother better now than I knew him when he was alive. It was almost like I was in Vietnam with him. I have attended almost every reunion for the past 21 years."

When asked if it gets more difficult or does she look forward to the reunions, Susan responded, "Oh, I look forward to them. I learn something new every time I go, a new picture, or I meet someone new. My girlfriend lost her brother in Vietnam, too. I met her online, and we started talking about it, and that was so helpful because we could bounce things off each other, kind of made us feel like we weren't crazy since every time we saw a photo of that black granite wall we'd be scanning the photo for our brother's names. Her name is Julie Kink. We even roomed together before we had husbands." (Susan giggled)

As if fate had put these two ladies together, Susan explained, "I have a picture of Julie and her brother's 'high bird'…he was flying 'high bird' when Mark was shot down. Her brother was Mark's wingman on the day Mark lost his life."

Struggling with *Dear Mark:* "I wrestled with the book because I was trying to tell a war story that I wasn't in, then someone suggested I write epistolary, so that's what I did, I wrote letters to Mark after he was gone, about going to the reunions, about meeting the men from his unit and learning what my brother was all about in Vietnam."

Discussing Susan's second book "*Through the Eyes of the Tiger.*" "Well, I was sitting around my aunt's and uncle's table and they were giving me telegrams and cards that my father had sent to his mother during WWII. I was turning the pages and I pulled a letter from an envelope that started out, 'Dear folks, if you're reading this don't be sad …..' and I thought, 'who writes a letter like that?' The letter was written by my dad's first cousin, John Donavan. John flew with the Flying Tigers and was killed while strafing the Hanoi Airport in 1942. (Japan occupied what was then called French Indochina—Vietnam—during WWII).

John would have been Mark's hero had Mark known about our dad's first cousin. John's plane was the only one lost on that mission to Hanoi, and he was shot down 1,000 kilometers from where Mark was shot down."

Her final thoughts: "I wrote *Dear Mark* to keep his legacy alive long after I'm gone so future generations will know about my brother and what he did for his country. He was proud of what he was doing and I couldn't be prouder of him. My purpose of the book was not really 'healing' because I think you never get over this kind of stuff, and it's not 'closure' as they say, I mean, he's still my brother and he was gone way too soon, but I feel like I have honored him by writing the book. Mark was a good guy."

In the foreword to *Dear Mark*, a Special Forces soldier speaks of how he's able to tuck his grandchildren in bed at night because of Mark's air support missions. Mark's name is forever etched into the black granite of The Wall, panel 22 west, line 57. One pilot, one son, one brother, one American hero among 58,318 heroes whose names are etched into one of the two 246 ft. 9 inch blocks of solid black granite.

Dear Mark is available at *deedspublishi*ng.com

Sybil Knox
Epitome Of The Home Front

Sybil Knox typifies the Home Front from the viewpoint of a southern clan deeply steeped in military tradition. Born Sybil Garner at home in Atlanta on Feb 8, 1923, the Girls High graduate married Ben Knox on July 28, 1941.

"We lived on Memorial Drive," she stated. "I remember the Sunday that Ben went to the store for some milk and came home with an apprehensive look on his face. I said, 'What's wrong?' He replied, 'Honey, the Japanese have attacked Pearl Harbor,' so we knew war was upon us. Our main worry was Ben's brother, Robert, who was stationed on Hickam Field in Hawaii."

On the morning of December 7, 1941, Sybil's brother-in-law, Robert Knox, slipped on his pants and stepped out of his tent to bask in the beautiful morning blue of Hawaii. Sybil relayed his story. "Nurses had arrived that week and were given the men's barracks for their quarters. The guys had to set up and live in Army tents. As Robert stepped out of his tent that morning, he spotted airplanes overhead and said to himself, 'the Navy pilots sure are out early this morning.' But as he continued to watch, one of the planes dropped what he thought was a wing tank. Then all the explosions started and Japanese planes strafed the field. One of Robert's buddies was cut in half by the strafing. The poor boy was missing his body from the waist down. Robert took his last request, 'You tell my momma I died a good boy'. Robert relayed those words months later to his buddies' parents. He said it was the toughest thing he'd ever done."

A lot of good boys die in war. An uncle of Sybil's mother, a man called Kinney, fought for the Confederacy during the Civil War. He died on the bluffs of Kennesaw and is buried atop the mountain. On Feb 15, 1898, a massive explosion blew apart the USS *Maine* in Havana Harbor with the loss of 260 men, an incident resulting in The Spanish-American War. The *Maine*, a modern battleship for its era, had been part of America's Great White Fleet, so-called due to their shark white hulls. The battleship circumnavigated the globe as a gesture of goodwill yet displayed American sea power. Sybil's father-in-law was aboard the *Maine*. Her father, Roy Garner, attended Officer Candidate School in Chamblee before serving in WWI.

During the Great Depression and WWII, Sybil's father provided for his family as a fire fighter. On Dec 7, 1946, exactly five years after the bombing of Pearl Harbor, Fire Captain Roy Garner and his unit responded to a blaze that entered a sad chapter in Atlanta's history: the infamous Winecoff Hotel fire. She said, "Dad's unit was the second on scene. It was dreadful; 119 dead and dozens injured. My father stayed all day and all night then entered the hotel the next morning to search for even more victims. He found five people in a room on the top floor playing cards. They had used wet blankets and sheets to seal off the doors and windows and had no idea of the scope of the tragedy on the bottom floors. That miracle got to my father; he broke down and cried."

After Pearl Harbor, Sybil's husband donned a uniform to serve his country. "We discussed his options," she said. "He didn't want to wait to be drafted so he enlisted in the Army Air Corps. He and his boss at the Georgia Power Company joined the same day at Fort MacPherson in April of '42."

Ben Knox trained at Kessler Field in Alabama and tested potential pilots at several locations, spending his final 14 months in El Paso. Sybil said, "By then Ben's acute sinus problems resulted in a medical discharge. Our first child was due in two weeks and there we were in El Paso, Texas facing a train trip back to Atlanta. I figured our first child was destined to be born in a Pullman car, but we made it home and I gave birth less than two weeks later."

Sybil's younger brother, James Garner, witnessed the war firsthand. I talked to James via Sybil's cellphone. He recalled, "I served with the Merchant Marines for five or six months then joined the Navy. Due to my sea-going experience, the Navy put me in charge of a five-man landing craft aboard the AKA-84 Attack Transport USS *Waukesha*. Later in the war we picked up Marines on Saipan and assisted in the invasion of Okinawa."

Off of Okinawa, the *Waukesha's* 20mm and 40mm anti-aircraft guns kept the Japanese suicide planes (Kamikazes) at bay. James said, "The Kamikazes came at us at all hours, day and night. We were always at combat stations. I saw Kamikazes hit several of our ships." After the Japanese announced their surrender, the *Waukesha* was one of the first American combat ships to enter Tokyo Bay. "The Japanese gun emplacements at a narrow channel were marked with white flags," James said. "Good lord, I'd never seen so many white flags in my life!"

After the formal surrender, the *Waukesha* dropped off Marines and telecommunications gear then set sail for Nagasaki, the target of the second atomic bomb dropped on Japan. James recalled, "The picture is etched in my brain; I'll never forget the sight. The destruction was total, nothing left but a few smoke stacks. Bodies were everywhere, the stench overwhelming."

Sybil's two grandsons are in the military as of this writing. She said proudly, "Brandon has been in the Navy for over 15 years serving with and now supervising catapult crews. He's served on the aircraft carriers *Eisenhower* and *Stennis*. My other pride and joy grandson, Aaron, graduated cum laude from North Georgia College as the seventh highest ranking cadet in the nation. Aaron is presently serving with the Army in Korea as a 1st Lieutenant."

Sybil commented on Tom Brokaw's best-selling book, *The Greatest Generation*. "Well, I read his book. It was a nice tribute to our generation, but in truth all of us did what we had to do. You know, as a kid I didn't realize the horrors of the Great Depression. I had food to eat, stayed warm, and I was loved. We didn't have 'things' but 'things' don't make you happy, your attitude does.

"I'd like to say just one more thing. During World War Two I was employed by the H. G. Hastings Seed Company. We sent Bermuda grass to occupied islands in the Pacific but I never knew why. And I remember riding the trolley to and from work and seeing all the Army convoys with the trucks loaded with young men on their way to war. They'd smile, whistle at the pretty girls, they seemed so cheerful, but I always wondered how they really felt, and I wondered how many of those boys would make it home. I said a prayer for every convoy."

Teresa "Terri" Prieto
Turn On The TV; We're Under Attack

The Vietnam War is credited with the distinction and/or ignominy of being the first American war viewed on television by the general public. Parents and loved ones actually saw the pain in their sons' or brothers' or husbands' face as a corpsman patched his wounds or damaged limbs. One persistent rumor claimed one mother saw her son die on the small screen, but evidence is lacking.

Americans saw bombs being dropped, napalm scorching the earth, aircraft carriers burning from accidental detonations on the flight deck, pilots and other POWs paraded through the streets of Hanoi, and flag-draped coffins loaded and unloaded with the remains of young men that lost their lives in one of America's most unpopular conflicts.

The Tet Offensive of '68 shocked the nation into believing the war was lost when in fact the US military crushed the Viet Cong into non-existence and so badly devastated their allies, the North Vietnamese Army, that it took a full two years for the NVA to recover. It mattered little. The news media, including the venerated CBS correspondent Walter Cronkite, tossed in the towel, soon to be followed by the populace.

Thrown into the puzzling mix of confusion and slanted news reporting was the shockwave that traumatized the world when Civil Rights leader Martin Luther King, Jr. was assassinated on April 4, 1968. The efforts of American soldiers thundering out of their base camps to defeat the communist forces in conclusive battles became back page news as American cities burned and the distaste of Martial Law ruled the land.

John Kennedy, Martin Luther King, Jr., and Bobby Kennedy fell for their causes, just like the boys in Vietnam. Their assassinations, along with a war fought half-ass by political leaders in Washington, DC, shaped an enduring legacy for the 1960s, an era of death and destruction and division, all played out on small screens in millions of dens and living rooms throughout our great nation.

The worst was yet to come, or more appropriately, yet to be televised.

On September 11, 2001, Americans saw a war started on their television sets. We got hit, hard, and our nation was stunned that the vast Pacific Ocean and The Pond no longer protected our shores. Much like December 7, 1941, we failed to heed the warnings and failed to disseminate the telltale Intelligence. Even more outrageous, a terrorist organization called Al Qaeda led by Saudi Osama Bin Laden had declared war on the United States and we essentially dusted off the threat like dandruff on a shoulder.

The words 'too cocky' come to mind, but Monday morning quarterbacking is a sport best left for the conspiracy buffoons. America got caught with its pants down. The resulting embarrassment and anger caused hasty decisions and Intelligence miscalculations on what, who, and where were we were going to kill in revenge. Almost 20 years later, we're still killing. This is not a War on Terror or an Overseas Contingency Operation; America is in a long drawn-out Holy War. If or when we quit killing, the killing will return to our own shores.

As we watched the Twin Towers fall, saw part of the Pentagon crumble, and witnessed smoke billowing above Shanksville, PA, most of us observed the catastrophe from the comfort of our homes or workplaces. But for those that were there, for those who suffered and saw friends die, and for those who survived, their perception of the televised disaster was not a small screen event. Theirs was and remains a lifelong homage to their colleagues and coworkers, the first-responders and firemen, and the courageous passengers that gave their all.

Teresa "Terri" Prieto was at the Pentagon on September 11, 2001 when hi-jacked American Airlines Flight 77 hurtled into the west side of the building. Sixty four passengers and crew members were killed instantly, plus another 125 military and civilian personnel perished inside the Pentagon.

Prieto said, "Four of the casualties were my friends. When I close my eyes, it's like it happened yesterday." Seven years passed before she penned her narrative of the tragedy; talking about it took a lot longer.

Her journey began in high school when an Army recruiter stirred her interest in the military. A Florida native, Prieto recalled, "After graduation I drove to Tampa for the physical and to begin the processing, but that's as far as I got." Laid off from her civilian accounting job in 1991, interest in the Army resurfaced. She explained, "I pounded the pavement looking for work and I refused to accept unemployment. I wanted a job, not charity; and I knew the Army had plenty of jobs. I enlisted after discussing the options with my first husband."

She took basic training and attended school for Personnel at Fort Jackson, SC. In July, '92, Prieto boarded a chartered airliner and flew non-stop to Rhein-Main AFB in Frankfurt, Germany. There she processed evaluation reports on officers and enlisted men at the 5th Corp Personnel Center in the Abrams Headquarters Complex. Prieto remembered, "My daughter and husband joined me in September. We moved into on-base housing and my daughter attended the American school. My husband found work at the PX across the street from our base. The commissary had a Popeye's Chicken, Burger King, and Chi Chi's Mexican Restaurant. We thought it strange that the McDonald's in Germany served beer but charged for ketchup." During her deployment the family visited Paris, ate at the Moulin Rouge café, scaled the Eiffel Tower, explored Adolf Hitler's Eagles Nest in Berchtesgaden, and defied death on the German Autobahn.

Prieto's appointment with destiny inched closer after being assigned to Fort Myer, Virginia next to Arlington National Cemetery. Even though she'd reenlisted, Prieto knew her military days were coming to an end. She said, "In Germany I was diagnosed with Morton's Neuroma, a podiatric disease caused by the lack of fat cells in the feet. I was basically rubbing bone on bone when marching or jogging. I cried from the pain." She underwent surgery to cut the nerves in her feet to ease the discomfort. "It didn't help much," Prieto stated.

Still battling Morton's Neuroma, Prieto jumped at the opportunity when offered a civilian position as a computer consultant for a private contractor inside the Pentagon. She said, "The Army allowed lateral moves, so I left the military and started working in the Pentagon the next day."

The Pentagon has five floors, five sides, and five rings. The rings start in the interior as A and B, separated from outer rings C, D, and E by an avenue for truck deliveries. The outer E ring was targeted on 9/11.

Astonishingly, the first news of the attack for Prieto arrived via email. She recalled, "One of my friends emailed me and said the Pentagon was on fire; I didn't believe her. I was on the opposite side of the building and didn't feel the impact. About that same time my supervisor received a call and was told a helicopter had struck the west E ring. He bolted out of the building and then security personnel began emergency evacuations. My coworker and I tried to swipe our cards to leave but a security officer shouted, 'Don't swipe, just get outa here!', so we ran from the building to a grassy area on the other side of the parking lot. We saw huge pillars of smoke billowing from the west E ring. That's when I knew it wasn't a helicopter that hit the Pentagon."

Although confused and terrified, Prieto said Pentagon personnel felt a sense of comfort when fighter jets arrived overhead. "We were glad to see the jets because security officers were yelling, 'Move back! Move back! Another plane is inbound!' That was the airliner that went down in Shanksville but I doubt if anybody that day actually knew where it was headed."

Prieto was told to go home. "I fought awful traffic jams, picked up isolated or stranded families, and I tried to call home," she stated. "But cell phones were useless because of overloaded airwaves." Eventually able to reach all of her family members, Prieto returned to work on 9/12 as fear and sadness gripped the nation.

"I was proud to see the American flag draped over the side of the Pentagon; it was like our country was saying, 'they only won the first round.' And by the way, one of my friends saw the plane hit the Pentagon so the conspiracy freaks need to get a life!"

Prieto and all of her coworkers noticed that the vending machines had been vandalized, or so they thought. "We found out the firemen and other rescue personnel had broken into the machines on 9/11 for the soft drinks in order to stay hydrated and give fluids to the survivors."

Terri Prieto kept her memories bottled up for years. She was a survivor as well as a victim. Happy to be alive, she still questions why so many friends paid the ultimate price for being an American while she was spared. Stress and nightmares plague her to this very day. "It's getting easier," she stated during the interview. "But I will never get over 9/11. We weren't the men and women that saw the attack on TV, we were the ones that experienced a national tragedy first hand, saw it, smelled it, breathed it, and lived to tell the tale. We will never forget 9/11. I hope our country doesn't either."

Prieto now works and lives in Georgia with her second husband, Bill Prieto, and two step-daughters. They attend Epiphany Lutheran Church where she serves as a Stephen Minister. When asked her final thoughts, she said, "It's strange what comes to your mind after all these years, but I hark back to the hot dog stand in the middle of the Pentagon's courtyard, with five sides and a pointed roof. For several years the Soviet Union thought it was a ballistic missile silo."

"What a cruel thing is war: to separate and destroy families and friends, and mar the purest joys and happiness God has granted us in this world; to fill our hearts with hatred instead of love for our neighbors and to devastate the fair face of this beautiful world."

General Robert E. Lee, in a letter to his wife, Christmas Day, 1862.

Victoria Collier
A Bundle Of Dynamite

Victoria Collierv

She is nationally recognized among lawyers as 'the' veteran's pension expert, yet eldercare attorney Victoria concentrates most of her attention on the older generation. "I help older people obtain access to quality care in their Golden Years," she proudly stated. "I love working with seniors and supporting their endeavors to find all those 'loopholes' hidden from the people who have earned that valuable attention."

Her expertise as an eldercare attorney began as a youthful journey of independence, to military carpentry, paralegal cross-training, a tattoo, then years of undergraduate and law school studies. All that energy is packaged into a 100 lb. 5'3" bundle of dynamite, with untiring devotion and, when needed, pit bull fervor.

A Houston, TX native, Victoria left home after high school for the Dallas- Fort Worth area to pursue her future. "That didn't work out very well," she recalled. "I didn't even know how to change a fuse, much less know what a fuse box was. I learned to take care of myself, fix a cabinet door or change a flat tire, and had my first exposure to eldercare working for a nursing home."

Within a year she realized formal training and education opened more doors than independence. "I enlisted in the Air Force when I was 19," she said. "During basic training at Lackland AFB we were given dream sheets and tests for placement. I wanted to fly as a cargo master but although I could lift a specified weight, I couldn't lift it high enough because of my height. My first choice after that, believe it or not, was carpentry. I wanted to be outside. Desk jobs for Air Force women at the time required skirts and blouses; listen, that's not me. I was given a photo of a flathead screwdriver...I identified it as a Phillips Head. Not a great start, but I was still given my first choice, carpentry. I also filled out the sheet for a choice of duty stations. I specifically requested no overseas duty and a base on the East Coast." She was sent straight to Germany.

Ramstein, Germany: "I was called a Structural Specialist, a part of Civil Engineering," Victoria stated. "Much like Navy Seabees, but Air Force. We maintained the air base, housing, roofing, hangars, the big rollup doors, and created office spaces using a special interior plaster. I liked it; thought it was pretty neat, and had no fear climbing up on house or hangar roofs. Call us handymen, that's okay, I enjoyed it. In Germany, the doors would lock behind you so I did a lot of 'breaking in' for folks, too," she said, smiling.

Working in a shop of 50 guys and one other woman presented challenges for the 'new kid'. She said, "It was rough on me at first, being small and female, plus the other woman wouldn't talk to me. I didn't have much to do, so just did my best, until I overheard the front line supervisor say that I was lazy. No way, that's not me. So I stayed under his feet, with a broom, a mop, anything and everything to prove myself. It worked. I was accepted by my peers and my assignment in Germany turned out to be a wonderful experience."

Victoria participated in Volksmarches (people 'fitness' marches). She explained, "Those were long walks we took with the citizens. After so many kilometers there would be shots of some kind of alcohol waiting for us to keep us warm, or at least that's the excuse they used. After walks or other activities, people would shower coed, well, that's not me either, but you do get used to it, sort of."

Asked if she picked up the language, Victoria replied. "A little. I knew enough German to ask for a restroom key or get directions. I pulled into a service station area once and told the attendant I was looking for the Black Forest. He answered, 'Lady, you're in it.' Language barrier or not, Germany is a beautiful country."

After two years of periodic Volksmarches, climbing roofs, building office space and maintaining rollup doors and hangars, Victoria headed home to the Lone Star State. "I was sent to Dyess AFB near Abilene," she said. "I did the handyman bit for about a year then decided I wanted out of the Air Force. A friend told me to cross-train instead of getting out. So I chose a tech school for paralegals. I took tests and had interviews and apparently had what the Air Force wanted."

Paralegal tech school was in Biloxi, MS. "That started my interest in the legal profession," she said. "I enjoyed tech school, learned a lot, and of course in tech school you're supposed to get a tattoo. So I did." Asked to show her tattoo, Victoria grinned and replied, "Well, it's a heart but showing it to you would be inappropriate."

To relieve the stress of school, plus have a little fun, Victoria and three other airmen decided a trip to the Mardi Gras made perfect sense. "I don't know if it made any sense at all," she admitted. "I'm not much of a drinker, not at all, but at some point I joined another group, partied a bit too much, then they went home. I found myself alone at 3:00am in an alley among some really scary dregs. I hailed a taxi but had trouble remembering the name of our hotel, so told the driver our hotel had a fountain outside. He responded, 'Lady, every hotel in New Orleans has a fountain out front.' Well, somehow he found the right one. That was my last escapade to Mardi Gras."

Victoria remained in the Air Force as a paralegal for another three years but the passion for law pulled her out of the military into college, with a law degree as the final goal. Her first port-of-call was Valdosta State to earn a degree in Psychology. Next, the University of Nebraska to earn a law degree. With her mom, dad, and a sister living in Atlanta, plus fond of big city opportunities, Victoria moved to Decatur in 2002 and opened a law practice.

A strong advocate for the elderly, she also represents veterans for non-service connected disabilities. Victoria stated, "My goals with veterans are very simple: to let them improve their pensions with three levels of aid and assistance. One, letting them know this assistance exists. Two, to help them obtain home care from the Veterans Administration. Three, using the laws to their advantage, finding those infamous 'loopholes' to do the right thing."

Victoria Collier is the real deal. "I love working with seniors," she said. "As we discussed, I worked with critical care seniors in a nursing home before I joined the military. During my stint in the Air Force, I worked off base at night in home healthcare. This is who I am."

When asked if military service helped her prepare for the future, she replied, "Absolutely. I have a much better affinity towards veterans. The military is a community like no other. You miss it when you're not in, so representing and being with veterans is like being back in, so to speak. The veterans of World War Two and Korea are very special to me. Vietnam veterans are different; they're not quite old enough, not yet. No affront meant, but it's the legal issues of the older people that attract me. I joined the military when I was 19 years old and I'm glad I did. In the military you see things and form lasting relationships. You don't have to worry if they have your back, you know they do because you have theirs. I don't know of any other community like that."

Considering her exposure to other cultures and other countries while in the military, she responded, "You learn to appreciate the United States of America. And let me say this; I appreciate blue collar workers. Estate planners use tax codes to help the rich avoid paying their taxes yet we need taxes to fund programs for the poor. The blue collar worker, the middle class if you will, pays for it all yet can't gain access to the funds of the rich or take advantage of programs for the poor. Blue collar folks built this county; it's who we are, it's who I am."

Her final thoughts: 'Yes, and please quote me. I believe I'm serving my country more now by helping senior veterans than when I served as an enlisted person." Victoria's Elder & Disability Law Firm can be reached at: victoria@elderlawgeorgia.com

Virginia Hooten Lott
God Was Good To Us

"I just came by to tell you men how much I appreciate your service to our

country. My husband was wounded on two Jima, so I understand the cost of freedom." This heartfelt recognition is repeated each month to our Veteran's Brunch at Merryvale Assisted Living in Covington by a true Southern Belle of a lady, Mrs. Virginia Hooten Lott. We call her Miss Virginia.

Personality Plus, best describes her spunk and spirit, and I knew a story of love and sacrifice resided in her heart. Little did this journalist know that her home front narrative would open the door to one of the most remarkable untold accounts of World War II. If made into a movie, I'll volunteer to write the screenplay. Born and raised in Covington, when asked her birthdate, Miss Virginia replied with a smile, "Now, that's not something you ask of a lady."

Married without her parent's knowledge at the age of 16 to Fred Lott, Miss Virginia and her husband would travel a familiar path of the Greatest Generation, one of service, sacrifice, and rebuilding their lives after a worldwide crusade.

"Fred joined with his two brothers; Fred the Army, Henry the Navy, and Herbert the Marines," Miss Virginia said. "I guess they figured joining three different branches would offer a better chance of at least one returning home."

Miss Virginia joined her husband briefly during his training in Texas and his first posting in California. "Fred was in charge of an anti-aircraft unit protecting the West Coast," she said. "But it wasn't long before he was sent to Seattle for deployment in the Pacific."

Pregnant with their first child, Miss Virginia traveled home to Georgia to live with her parents and to await the return of her husband. That Fred Lott did return from the Pacific is something of a miracle.

The words of Fred Lott, Jr: "Dad didn't talk much about the war but I know he was in charge of a half track with a 20mm anti-aircraft gun and a seven man crew. He and his crew saw action in the Palau

Island Group (better known as the Battle of Peleliu Island) and I know at one point they were in hand-to-hand combat. After that fight, Dad hit a couple more islands before his last battle."

Fred Lott survived his last battle on a speck of an island called Iwo Jima. Sent ashore with a half track and gun crew, the following pieces of the story are recollections by Miss Virginia and her son, Fred, Jr:

Miss Virginia: "My husband and his men arrived on Iwo Jima as the flag was raised atop Mount Suribachi. Fred said there was great joy by the ground troops and ships at sea upon seeing the Stars and Stripes flying over the island. Moments later they hit a land mine."

Fred, Jr: "Moments after the flag raising, Dad's half-track hit a ground rocket (a land mine crafted from a Japanese artillery shell). All his men were killed; Dad was the only survivor."

Now an extraordinary quirk of fate and the unpredictable nature of war reunited three brothers. The odds must be astronomical, but this is the story:

Fred Lott's back was broken and his chest shattered. Evacuated to one of four LST-H ships (large LST landing craft converted into hospital ships, each with four surgeons and 27 corpsmen), he was stabilized and shipped to one of the larger hospital ships, either the USS Samaritan AH-10 or USS Solace AH-5. Aboard the larger hospital ship was Corpsman Henry Lott, Fred's brother. Although in critical condition, Fred talked with his brother before being sent for additional medical treatment in Saipan, Guam, or perhaps the Mariana Islands.

Meanwhile, on Iwo Jima, Marine Herbert Lott received a million dollar' wound that got him off the island onto a hospital ship, the same ship on which his older brother had received treatment and the other brother, Henry, served as a corpsman. The Lott family is not sure if Henry and Herbert met aboard the hospital ship, but fate did save all three brothers from the indispensable cost of freedom, all three at the same place and time in one of the most horrific battles of WWII.

After intensive research, I could not find another occasion during WWII where three brothers serving in three different branches of the service became united during the same battle at the same time. This is truly one of the best kept untold secrets of WWII.

After a lengthy hospitalization in Hawaii, Fred Lott eventually returned to Georgia and remained in a body cast for 13 months in a military hospital, either in Savannah or Milledgeville. He wore a back brace for two years.

Miss Virginia: "It was difficult to visit Fred since gasoline was rationed, but we did the best we could. Herbert had recovered from his wounds and was home, too. Herbert managed to find enough gas for us to visit Fred on occasion. Fred, Jr. was one year old before my husband saw his face. My husband suffered with back pain all his life but after ten years of rehabilitation he found employment at the Covington Post Office and worked alongside his brother, Herbert."

"God was good to us," Miss Virginia continued. "We had a full life and raised three children, Fred, Jr., Susan, and Nancy. We were grateful for jobs and a good life. Fred retired from the post office and also served as the Commander of the American Legion. I worked in banking."

Miss Virginia's humble statement does not reflect her brilliant career at the Bank of Covington: Starting in March of 1957, Miss Virginia worked as a filing clerk, teller, branch manager, bank vice-president, and branch coordinator until retirement in 1989 — 32 years serving the people and community of Newton County. "I loved every minute of it," she said.

Her final thoughts: "I was a member of the home front and it was hard waiting on your man to come back from war. I wrote him a letter every day and he wrote me when he could. But I had great support from my family and friends. We had a good life." When asked if I could take her picture, Miss Virginia said, "No, I'm not properly dressed and I haven't done my hair this morning." Thanking her for the interview and offering an apology for asking her age at the beginning of our talk, Miss Virginia replied with a grin, "I appreciate the apology; I'll be 90 in October."

Tonia Ann George – Teufel-Hunden
The Outpost Bar & Grill

During the Great War, later referred to as the First World War, the German soldiers at the Battle of Belleau Wood called their ruthless American opponents Teufel-Hunden, meaning 'Devil Dogs'. The 'Devil Dogs' are also called Leathernecks, Jarheads, and Gyrenes. Many units have adopted the mantra *Improvise, Adapt, and Overcome.* Of many possible etymologies, *'Oorah'* is the most common. They greet each other with *'Semper Fi',* which is short for their motto, *'Semper Fidelis'* (Always Faithful). And there are no former or ex-members, since *'Once a Marine, Always a Marine.'*

An MOS (Military Occupational Specialty) '0311-Basic Rifleman' is as Marine as you can get, meaning a 'grunt', a first in — first to die ground-pounder, a boots-on-the-ground badass. A 'Pogue' is not an infantryman, rather, a rear-echelon type MOS usually out of Harm's Way, a clerical or other type of cushy job, more commonly noted as 'in the rear, with the gear'. Call a Pogue an infantryman and he'll swell with pride; call a grunt a Pogue and, well, just be sure your medical insurance is current.

All the fun started on November 10, 1775, when Captain Samuel Nicholas was granted authorization by the Second Continental Congress to raise two battalions of Marines. He advertised in a newspaper for "A Few Good Men." 'One Good Woman' wasn't allowed until Opha

May Jacob Johnson joined the Marine Corps on August 15, 1918. Now, that said and done, all I wanted was a cold beer.

I walked into The Outpost at Honey Creek on November 10th of last year (2018) and found myself in a rather raucous elbow-to-elbow revelry celebrating the 243rd birthday of the U.S. Marine Corps. The Outpost Bar and Grill is pro-military, pro-American, and radiates the spirit of the Marine Corps, which echoes the owner's background as a Marine veteran. Veterans, along with a swarm of America-loving folks, bellied-up to the bar or a floor table for a cold brew or toddy and most likely the best bar food I've ever overeaten.

Two Marines were in uniform, nightcaps in hand and a smidgen of birthday cake in the corners of their mouths. The employees were scrambling to provide the service The Outpost is famous for while the owner, a feisty no-nonsense lady Marine veteran, played hostess and on one isolated occasion around midnight, the resident peacemaker. In all honesty, The Outpost is a bar for 'adults only' after the sun sets, so be forewarned: This is not an establishment to disrespect Old Glory, the military, or tender an opinion based on anti-American rhetoric. It's my kind of bar. On the other hand, as a journalist and veterans advocate, I took advantage of a superb opportunity to conduct my first 'inside a bar' interview, three to be precise, and these are the stories.

Note: The two male Marines, Steven Lamar Teague and Larry Whisenand, will have their day in another upcoming book, but this tome features lady warriors. Therefore, the following story reflects the experiences of The Outpost's owner, U.S. Marine and proprietor, Tonia Ann George.

"Hey, if you want a real Marine you need to interview me!" Her comment was aimed more at the two male Marines than yours truly, all in fun and camaraderie. A native of Osceola, Arkansas, feisty but all-business, Ann, as the customers call her, joined the Marines before graduating from high school. "I joined with my best friend, a guy, under the 'buddy system' so we could stay together. We both had a really bad childhood, so the Marine Corps was an escape for both of us."

Your thoughts on Parris Island?

"Well, you live on a time frame, you're exhausted, you're humiliated, it's excruciating, but rewarding; discipline, honor, respect, yes, sir and no, sir…and beyond. The Marines break you down then build you back up."

And after basic?

"You know, as I mentioned, I never felt really good about myself due to a traumatic childhood, but becoming a U.S. Marine made me a very proud woman. I live as a Marine and I'll die as a Marine. My first, and only, assignment was Lemoore Naval Air Station just outside of Fresno, CA. That's near those beautiful giant Redwood trees. I was a guard, I guarded the base, and came out as an MP."

Aren't you a bit small for an MP?

"Well, I'm a badass. I was in Lemoore for six years and moved up in rank rapidly due to great test scores. I elected to take the difficult assignments; I wanted to prove my worth. I wish I could have stayed in the Marines."

Why did you leave?

"They found out I had Leukemia. I'm 32 years in remission, but I had to leave the Marines. The Marines worked with me, even promoted me to NCO status when I had to get out. I was also told if I wanted children, I'd better do it quickly. Well, my best friend and I fell in love and got married. I got pregnant but was really sick. My daughter was born lifeless, but she made it. An amazing girl. Well, I got pregnant again. Then my husband left for Desert Storm and I was down to 62 lbs., really, really sick a second time. But, my Marine training and the Good Lord got me through all this. Everything that has happened to me was a gift and made me the strong person I am today."

And you own The Outpost?

"Yeah, I bought the business from my present husband. We fell in love and got married."

When did you divorce your first husband?

"I didn't. He was killed in Desert Storm."

Sorry.

"Thanks. Yeah, I've been in the bar business going on 30 years, managed several of them, and they were all good to me. I've had 32 chemo treatments and 17 direct radiation treatments. Even when I was too sick to work they would bring paperwork to me so I could still get a paycheck.

Anyway, when we got married in 2014 I took over The Outpost the same year. We're doing well, these folks are my Outpost family. If one of us faces a problem, then we all come together to help. No stranger walks in here and leaves a stranger."

Your final thoughts?

"I have two wonderful daughters and nine grandchildren. I take care of business with a smile on my face, but if necessary, I can also kick ass. I hope you focus the story on the retired Marines, the people who spent their whole life defending this country. I love my country, but I'm sad to see what's going on these days. It's heartbreaking. I would like you to mention that when the hurricane came through Alabama we sent seven trucks of water to help those folks. We do the Toys for Tots Marine program at Christmas, we do food drives, and we stand up for each other and stick together at The Outpost. We've helped pay medical bills for some of our regulars, if necessary. On Thanksgiving, Christmas, and Easter I open my doors to our in-house family so they can share a meal, even provide clothes if one becomes homeless. Like I said, I live as a Marine and I'll die as a Marine."

Good people come from all walks of life, be it a bar or a Baptist church. We are all a part of the human race. Judge not, or lest ye be judged. As the adage recommends, "Walk a mile in my shoes." Good advice, but among Marines you'll hear the suggestion, "Walk a mile in my combat boots." *Improvise ... Adapt ... Overcome!*

Missing in Action
Coming Home – Part I

1st Lt. Michael Blassie

Mike was a spitting image of what most people believe a young Air Force officer should look like: tall, handsome, with a hospitable grin and approachable demeanor. A 1970 graduate of the Air Force Academy, he lettered on varsity tennis and soccer teams. In 1968 and 1969 Mike was nominated to the All-Rocky Mountain League Soccer Team. He studied psychology and in 1971 received his aeronautical rating after graduation from the Academy. After qualifying on A-37B Dragonfly (Super Tweet) Cessna attack aircraft, he was deployed to Vietnam to serve with the 8th Special Operations Squadron.

The 8th Special Operations Squadron is one of the oldest units in the United States Air Force, organized in 1917 at Camp Kelly, Texas. The unit fought on the Western Front in World War I, then called The Great War, and primarily flew the Dayton-Wright DH-4, a reconnaissance aircraft. The squadron fought and flew in the Pacific during World War II and served in Korea flying Douglas B-26 Invaders. During the Vietnam War, the unit flew the Martin B-57 Canberra medium bomber and in the closing years of the conflict changed over to the small but lethal Cessna A-37 Dragonfly, a light attack aircraft.

When Mike saddled-up to an A-37B Dragonfly at the Bien Hoa Airbase in Vietnam, he did so as a member of an air commando unit, which suggests to this old Intelligence guessaholic that he was flying covert missions into Laos and Cambodia. He also flew COIN (counter-insurgency) missions and served as a forward air controller. On May 11, 1972, while starting a bombing run on enemy artillery positions on the outskirts of An Loc near the Cambodian border, fellow airmen saw tracer rounds from ground fire coming up toward Mike's A-37B. The anti-aircraft rounds found their mark.

Major James Connally, his flight commander, described the tragic incident in a letter to Mike's parents, "Mike's plane was hit and began streaming fuel. He must have been killed instantly since he did not transmit a distress call of any kind. The aircraft flew a short distance on its own and then slowly rolled over, exploding on impact in enemy-held territory." Yet the fog of war relates another version, of how the Dragonfly had inverted (flying upside down) and that Mike ejected from the stricken aircraft. Nevertheless, flying at low altitude to drop napalm, doing so would have propelled him into the ground.

Whatever the case, other aircraft were dispatched to the area to provide cover for an Army chopper rescue team, all for naught. The enemy threw up what was described as a 'murderous hail of fire' which forced a cancelation of the recovery and/or rescue attempt. Mike had become another cold statistic of war, an MIA (Missing in Action). The following day an Air Force chaplain visited the home of Mike's parents in St. Louis to inform them their son had been killed in action, but his remains could not be recovered since he went down in enemy-held territory. That tragic explanation would be the same story Mike's grieving parents would hear for the next 26 years, a story that soon bore little truth.

About six months after the incident, a South Vietnamese Army patrol located the crash site. In close proximity, the patrol recovered six bone fragments, a Beacon radio, two compasses, an American flag, a parachute, remnants of a pistol holder, a one-man life raft, dog tags, fragments of a flight suit, a wallet with family pictures and an I.D. with the wording: 1st Lt. Blassie, Michael Joseph.

With the discovery of the crash site and personal effects, thus began a sequence of events that literally baffles the imagination. On November 2, 1972, Michael Blassie's remains were turned over to the mortuary in Saigon. As his I.D. indicated, Michael was 6' in height and weighed 200 lbs. By testing bone fragments using a controversial technique known as 'morphological approximation', the estimated age of the deceased was between 26 to 33 years. Mike was 24 years old at the time of his death, 'outside' of the so-called age bracket.

The height of the deceased was estimated to be between 65.2 inches and 71.5 inches. Mike stood at 72 inches. By using a single strand of hair found in the flight suit, tests indicated the decease's blood type was not type "A", the blood type recorded as Blassie's. Ignoring official chain-of-custody documents, the remains (bones) were reclassified and designated to be 'unknown.'

DNA testing was in its infancy at the time of Mike's death and the procedures of remains identification sometimes seemed like guesswork. Astonishingly, changing lab reports and closing cases, basically 'getting the job done' due to internal pressures, was not uncommon at the time. The techniques were 'completely worthless' according to many forensic experts and to estimate a victim's height by the 'morphological' method was later deemed 'impossible'.

Disputes over lab details on a plane shot down over Laos finally sparked an independent report commissioned by the Army. The findings: 'Morphological approximation' was 'not a logical nor correct technique.' The procedure was discontinued. The horror behind the findings meant the probability existed that undetermined numbers of American war dead may have been buried in the wrong graves. And as if adding salt to emotional wounds, the Blassie family in St. Louis was never told that Michael's aircraft had been found nor that his remains had been recovered. The 'unknown' remains were stored in the Army's Central Identification Laboratory under the file number X-26.

Congress passed a law in 1973 authorizing the Defense Department to bury a Vietnam Unknown at Arlington National Cemetery. Although a gravesite was prepared, it remained empty for eleven years. Under pressure from the Veterans of Foreign Wars and the American Legion, the Congress and the Reagan Administration collectively agreed to go ahead with a burial. The year was 1984, an election year.

The Secretary of the Army wanted the ceremony to take place on Veterans Day, November 11. However, as the political animals in Washington, DC always do, that date would be five days *after* the election and the political elite did not want to miss a public relations opportunity. The date for the interment was pushed back to May 28, 1984: Memorial Day. One set of remains was available: X-26.

At the time, Major Johnie Webb was in charge of the Central Identification Laboratory and was acquainted with the Blassie case. He also understood Washington politics. Presented with papers to sign confirming the X-26 remains would never be identified, Webb refused to sign. Even the senior anthropologist who developed the 'morphological approximation' technique, a man named Furue, sided with Webb to adamantly oppose the burial at Arlington. Major Webb was given six months by the Pentagon to identify the remains of X-26. If a positive I.D. was not made by the end of six months, Webb was ordered to sign the certification. On March 21, 1984, Webb reluctantly signed.

Then, according to Webb, he was ordered by Army HQ in the Pentagon to destroy any evidence linking Blassie to file X-26, including the personal artifacts from the crash site. Webb wrestled with mixed emotions, of doing the right thing versus following orders. It was 'the struggle of my life', according to Webb. Major Webb chose to do what he considered to be the proper course of action: he disobeyed orders, putting his military career in jeopardy plus running the risk of a court-martial, and hid Blassie's remains and crash-site artifacts where no one would ever find them ...in the casket with X-26.

On May 28, 1984, a Third Army Old Guard horse-drawn caisson bearing the remains of X-26 moved slowly along Constitution Avenue. Over a quarter million people lined the route to Arlington National Cemetery, a series of 21-gun salutes cracked sharply in the distance, and military bands played respectful music. Approximately 100 vets of the Vietnam War, some bearded, some pushing their brothers in wheelchairs, some wearing jungle hats and worn-out camouflaged fatigues, followed the parade.

A few remarks of President Ronald Reagan's emotional farewell: *"Today, we pause to embrace him and all who served so well in a war whose end offered no parades, no flags, and so little thanks. We write no last chapters. We close no books. We put away no final memories."* Placing a Medal of Honor on X-26's flag-draped casket, President Reagan concluded, *"Thank you, dear son, and may God cradle you in his loving arms."*

The Blassie family was not in attendance. They had no way of knowing the remains of X-26 were that of a son and brother, their loved one who was killed in action in Vietnam. They didn't even know Michael's aircraft had been found, his remains recovered, as were artifacts to prove the deceased flyboy was actually Michael Joseph Blassie.

Michael's younger sister, Patricia Blassie, was 13 years old when her brother, the oldest of five siblings, was listed as 'MIA, presumed dead' in Vietnam. She recalled, "My father served in Normandy during World War II and he never got over losing Michael. He and Michael were very close. Dad set up a little memorial in the basement and would go down there all the time and just sit."

Patricia Blassie joined the Air Force as an enlisted airman, she now holds the rank of Colonel (O-6). In Part II of 'Coming Home' she relates the Blassie family story, of the heartbreak, all the unanswered questions, and the final fight to have Michael 'returned home.'

Coming Home – Part II

Shot down in enemy-held territory while on a bombing run in Vietnam near An Loc, 1st Lt. Michael Blassie was listed as MIA (Missing in Action) and the body said to be unrecoverable. In reality, his remains were recovered almost six months after the crash, but 'misidentified' and labeled 'unknown' then stored away under the label X-26. In 1984, the remains of X-26 were interred at the Tomb of the Unknown in Arlington National Cemetery to symbolize the Vietnam War Unknown.

Under pressure from the Blassie family and members of the forensic community, the remains were disinterred in 1996 and finally identified through DNA testing to be the remains of 1st Lt. Michael Blassie. Patricia Blassie was just 14 years old when her big brother lost his life in Vietnam. In this Part II of 'Coming Home', she shares the families' story, the heartbreak, the frustration, and the long painful struggle to 'bring Michael home.'

In Patricia's own words, with limited editing for amplification:

"I was born on August 17, 1958 in St. Louis, MO. There were five siblings, with Michael the oldest. He was 10 years old when I was born, so now he'd be 71. He was the kind of big brother you looked up to, soft spoken, that big smile of his, and when he left for the Air Force Academy we were all so proud of him. I didn't understand everything that was going on about him attending the Academy, but it was so exciting. Mike sold newspapers as a young man, always working, playing soccer and tennis. We all loved to compete. My sister, Judy, was only three years younger than Michael, so she looked upon their relationship differently than I did. But it was always the five us, we were a unit.

A sibling photo — the early years. Back row, L to R — Judy, Michael, and Mary.
Front row, L to R — George and Patricia

"The last day we took him to the airport as he left for Vietnam, Michael looked back at us and waved. We had no idea that was the last time we'd ever see him. Of course mom and dad were concerned, they understood war; I didn't. I never dreamed I'd never see Michael again."

Tell the reader's about the day the chaplain came
to break the tragic news to the family.

"That day changed the Blassie family forever. It's just like in the movies, they come to your house; they tell you what they know or think they know, then they leave. Mike was 24 when he was killed, I was 14. I'd left school early that day and I looked out the window when I heard a car door slam. I thought, 'What is that?' I went into the backyard and waited, I mean, everything seemed so strange. A neighbor came over to get me, saying, 'Pat, you need to go inside.' So I did and knew something was horribly wrong. They said Michael had been killed. They had a letter from his flight leader, James Connally, who recapped what had happened. But not bringing the remains home…it was so sad, but we wanted to know the rest of the story. We wanted the entire truth, but they couldn't tell us that.

"Michael was participating in Operation Linebacker I, a very intense battle, and a lot of people were lost on the same day we lost Michael on May 11, 1972. The choppers did what they could, but couldn't get to Michael. I thought he was MIA, but the military claimed he was KIAB-NR—Killed in Action, Body not Recovered. We were told his plane was streaming fuel then inverted, no communication, Michael went down and the plane exploded. They saw no parachute, yet the artifacts eventually discovered were not burned, so maybe he did eject. I guess we'll never know. After the internment at Arlington, we discovered documents and we wanted DNA testing, but we were told the bones were probably so charred that the DNA test was not a possibility. But we persisted, and discovered the bones were not that charred.

"We called Major Webb (Major Johnie Webb was in charge of the Central Identification Laboratory in Hawaii at the time) and thanked him for what he did. He followed all the orders given him, except the order to destroy the documents and Michael's artifacts. Major Webb hid

Michael's file, X-26, in the casket, so thankfully Michael's records and artifacts were not destroyed."

The South Vietnamese patrol and American advisors found the remains six months after the crash, but the Blassie family did not know that for 26 years. What were your feelings?

"Very hurtful. We realized decisions were being made for our mom and dad. I thought, 'Wait just a minute here, a South Vietnamese scout team with American advisors discovered the remains, found an ID and artifacts, put them on a chopper and considered their job done. I don't care what happened, but the documents showed that patrol went into Michael's crash site to find him, and they did. But for whatever reason, the first bad decision was not telling the family. The government does not have the right to keep such information from the family.

"When I looked into all the documents and from my personal research, it was obvious that improper decisions were being made and all of a sudden Michael is the unknown representing the missing from the Vietnam War. So they finally took him off the shelf, file X-26, and for that I'm thankful. When I think about Michael sitting on that shelf from Oct of 1972 until 1984, it just blew me away. At least he went into a place of honor, the Tomb of the Unknown. Mike was serving once again with dignity and honor as the representative of the Vietnam War, but once we found out it was indeed Michael, he was no longer 'unknown'.

How did your parents handle all of this?

"When something like this happens in a family, and this is my personal point of view, this kind of thing can bring a family together or tear it apart. We never talked about it, there was not anything to talk about; Michael just didn't come home. My parent's marriage did not survive. I don't know if Michael's death was the main contributor to the failed marriage, but you grow apart sometimes during this kind of tragedy. My father went to his grave in 1991 not knowing the rest of his son's story."

That's so tragic.

"Yes, but it was our mother that looked at us and said, 'I want to bring my son home.' She faced criticism from people, but would look at them and say, 'But it's not your son.' I am really proud of my sisters, Judy and Mary, and my brother, George, he is the youngest, and we all agreed with mom. It was the right thing to do."

Your mother was criticized? Is that explainable?

"Going back in time, the way we treated Vietnam veterans, we did not honor them as a government and as a nation, and then the Vietnam Wall was built, but not by the government. Every war had an unknown, but as a family we wanted the remains in the Tomb to be disinterred. To many Vietnam veterans, it was pretty upsetting to have the Vietnam 'unknown' disinterred. I talked with many of them and they would say, 'But this is the one honor we received,' and the Blassie family was disrupting that honor. I would reply, 'All the Vietnam unknowns should be accounted for by the government.' I would remind them of that, and I'd tell them our family story. We'd go on TV saying that we wanted Michael home, but those were just soundbites. With the Vietnam veterans, I'd sit with them and explain that Michael was one of their brothers, and all of us wanted to bring all of the MIAs home. I'd also remind them that Michael was never an unknown soldier . . . he was made one."

I think it will be difficult for the readers to believe the military ordered the documents to be destroyed.

Major Webb followed his orders, except destroying Michael's documents and artifacts. People say, 'What about the other unknowns?' Well, there's nothing available to lead us to the other unknowns, not yet anyway. Michael's situation was an anomaly."

Did Michael's death spur you to join the Air Force?

"Four years after Michael's death when I was graduating from high school, some recruiters came to the school . . . I didn't have any direction and the family was lower-middle income, I didn't even know how to go about college. Mike always knew what he wanted, I didn't. The recruiters said if I joined the Air Force, I'd travel, get excellent training, and an education. I signed up the next day. In my 17 year old mind, that sounded like a good deal. I signed up with the Air Force since I knew the Air Force, or I should say, I was more familiar with Air Force. But until I joined up, I didn't know what it meant to serve, what it means to our nation, and what Michael really did for us, as did all our veterans and all those who went before us, but I grew into that mold."

Once in the Air Force, did you like what you were doing?

"I loved it. I got to travel so many places in the world I would never have been able to visit, I got a great education, I have a Master's Degree, and I was trained like no other. I'm grateful how God works in our lives. Sometimes we don't know what we don't know, what is the purpose in life? And the training I received in the Air Force, well, wow, and then I went into public affairs. You do certain things to get the mission done, and I tell you this, had I not had that training I would not have been able to help my family to finally bring Michael home. I will always be grateful to the Air Force for my training. It was difficult at times, working to have Michael returned home, very intense, and you get that feeling in your stomach like, 'Geezz, this is scary.' But you carry on."

Did you receive any flak from the Air Force or your superiors?

"I was at the Pentagon at the time with the rank of Captain. I told my leadership what was going on. One time I did wear my uniform for an interview and it was getting close to the time for the Pentagon to make a decision on Michael's disinterment. I was pulled in and told never to wear my uniform during an interview. You see, when I'm in uniform, I'm speaking for the Air Force, and that was a difficult day for the Air Force. I don't feel that I was held back, my career was still going on, I was up for Major, but Michael was more important than my ranking."

Did the Air Force ever say anything to you about Michael? Did they offer you support?

"No, I don't recall anything like that. I know when we brought Michael home to St. Louis, four to five thousand people lined the streets and showed up for the funeral. Family friends and Michael's friends were there. Michael's flight leader, James Connally was there, as was Bill

Parnell who was with the South Vietnamese patrol and had kept Michael's remains overnight. They wanted to see the job done, they wanted Michael to be honored. No, I don't recall any congratulatory call or comment from the military."

George Blassie on right, escorting his brother home 26 years after
he was killed in Vietnam, photo taken in July of 1998

And where is Michael's final resting place?

"At Jefferson Barracks in St. Louis, it's a National Cemetery. We wanted Michael home, and we were serious about it."

Are you still in the military?

"I retired a year ago in July of 2018, after almost 40 years in the uniform. I served as enlisted for 11 years, earned a degree, then received my commission in 1989. I served as an officer from 1989 until 2018, retiring as a full bird Colonel. I wouldn't trade my enlisted years for anything. My initial goal was Chief Master Sergeant, you know, a Commander Chief. I had a Chief Master Sergeant tell me getting a commission was what I needed to do, he said I had the potential and to 'go for it.' I'm thankful I made that decision, and I'm thankful the Air Force had the confidence in me. I started out in supply as an enlisted airman, then cross-trained into public affairs.

This is a unique story. The Blassie family and Michael's story will go down in history.

"I realize that, and that's why I feel a responsibility to continue to tell Michael's story and to share it with others. I didn't ever expect this to happen to our family, none of us did. But I was thinking, 'It's not what happens, but what you do with what happens.' I believe my family did the right thing, and Mike is home."

Your final thoughts:

"I think about Michael often. He has come to the forefront in so many ways. I know had he lived, he would have mentored me and taught me in so many different ways. But in his death, his service, and what occurred with his selection to serve in the Tomb for 14 years representing Vietnam, well, Michael's story is never ending and always changing. I continue to grow with the changing dimensions. You know, when the family discussed what to do about Michael, my brother George said, "It's really an honor where Michael is buried, it's sacred ground…but he's a hero, and he deserves to be known." That really stuck with me, 'What's in a name,' a name, it's the very first thing we say in introduction. I will always remember what a Navy Seal said to me, 'Pat, what do we veterans put on our tombstones? Our name, our service, and what years we served. That defines your brother.' Your name, that is so important. I'm grateful for what Mike taught me in life, and, yes, in his death. Thank you for allowing me to share his story with your readers."

Note: As a Vietnam veteran and Air Force veteran, the story of Michael Blassie touched a tender spot deep within my soul. A 24 year old flyboy who was shot down in a war, 10,000 miles from home, and whose remains stayed in limbo for 26 years, was finally returned home to St. Louis, MO. It's hard to fathom the misidentification, the remains sitting on a shelf labeled X-26 as if a secret formula existed, and orders to destroy all artifacts and documents. Yet ethical people, both military and civilian, did the right thing at the right time. Doing 'the right thing' is always 'the best thing.' I earnestly hope and pray that 1st Lt. Michael Joseph Blassie is now and forever will be, Resting in Peace.

The Clubmobile Girls

Due to the ingenuity and can-do attitude of Yanks in WWII, the British witnessed several of their London Lorries remodeled into odd-looking Clubmobiles that smelled of coffee and donuts. In July and August of 1944, brand-new Clubmobiles crossed the stormy English Channel as remodeled 2½ ton Army trucks. These vehicles also smacked of hot Joe and circular pastry. Eventually 80 Clubmobiles and 320 females known as 'Clubmobile Girls' braved the hazards of war to provide our soldiers with familiar tastes and a touch of home. Fifty-two of the ladies would die in the line of duty.

'Clubmobile Girls' had to meet certain criteria: some college, a pleasant personality, and attractiveness. Their requirements toughened during the Korean and Vietnam Wars: a college degree, exhibit high moral standards, attractiveness, the gift of gab, and a knack for smiling when you wanted to weep. Most GIs in all three wars called these dedicated Red Cross workers Donut Dollies.

Mary Atkinson Robeck

Mary Atkinson Robeck grew up in Cajun Country a few feet below sea level in a city called New Orleans, better known as Nawlins'. A B.A. degree was attained at William Carey College in Hattiesburg, MS, then Mary continued studies at the University of Southern Mississippi for a Master's Degree in Sociology.

"I always wanted an unusual life, a life of service," Mary said. "In grad school I saw an ad for the Red Cross. They needed workers in military hospitals and for service in Vietnam. In the fall of 1970 I flew to Atlanta for an interview. I qualified, then requested the first opening in a military hospital as a social or recreation worker in the Southeast. I went home and told my parents the furthest posting would be North Carolina. So I waited; I waited for months. I was in the middle of tests and finishing my thesis for a Master's when I asked God, "Lord, make something happen."

Ask, and ye shall receive. Three days later Mary received a phone call from the Red Cross. Instead of a posting to a stateside military hospital, the Red Cross asked if Vietnam was an option for consideration. Mary recalled, "I agreed immediately. Since I had asked God to do something it seemed like the right thing to do."

She had two weeks to get things in order, finish and turn in her thesis, get all her shots and a passport, say goodbye to friends and family. "I am not a courageous person and have a deadly fear of heights," Mary said. "So the people in my hometown were stunned by my decision, and my parents were absolutely horrified. My mother was so desperate to talk me out of it, she said, 'You know there's not going to be enough water; you're not going to be able to wash your hair everyday like you love to do.' They thought I'd lost my mind." Her salary: $7,000 a year.

First stop, Atlanta: "So, I'm sitting in a hotel room in Atlanta waiting to travel to Washington, DC for training, and thinking, 'What have

I done?' Then suddenly I'm in Washington at the Red Cross National Headquarters; I'm walking to class in snow, learning military protocol and ranks, Red Cross history, proper conduct...it was exciting. The drug enforcement folks came to our class and actually burned marijuana so we'd recognize the smell. We had the reputation of the Red Cross on our shoulders so we didn't want to be in a situation to embarrass the organization or ourselves."

January, 1971: "We landed at Tan Son Nhut AFB in Saigon at 0400 in the morning. Dark, hot, steamy, welcome to Vietnam. I was amazed during the drive to the hotel to see refugees living in boxes or tin sheds. Inside our hotel I saw South Vietnamese soldiers sleeping in the lobby. After we got into a room I told my roommate, Ilene, how nice it was of the hotel to let the soldiers sleep in the lobby. Ilene said, 'Mary, you're an idiot. Those soldiers are supposed to be guarding the hotel.'"

"The next morning a lady came in from the field to train us for a week about what to do or not to do, the ins and outs of Vietnam. Then we were on our way to Qui Nhon on a C-130. Problem was, Qui Nhon was aflame in riots. Apparently a kid had been hit by an Army truck and the people had turned violent. However, we landed safely then a Red Cross lady came to get us and took us to her room until things calmed down a bit. So, we're sitting in this room when all of a sudden a woman runs in, says, 'Hello, I'm Susan Frankhart, your unit leader, there's a chopper waiting, let's go,' and we were gone that quickly."

"We didn't have time to think or worry. We got on the chopper, took off, dropped off a wounded ARVN soldier at the hospital then flew on to the Quincy Compound across town from Qui Nhon. We had a rec hooch called the 'Happy Hooch' where G.I.s could play pool or ping pong, drink Kool-Aid and eat popcorn. We didn't have donuts, it was just too hot and humid. I quickly learned that two girls worked the Happy Hooch while the rest went out to fire support bases, landing zones, raid bases, and we flew into Phu Cat to visit MACV teams outside the base. We flew into Pleiku often and into An Khe which by that time was basically a MASH unit."

The Donut Dollies minus the donuts, called their chopper runs Missions. Mission 1, perhaps An Khe, mission 2, to Phu Cat, mission 3, to Pleiku, etc. Recreational programs for the troops included classes and studies on camping, US Presidents, even cheese. Remarkably, many of the soldiers studied before their classes on program topics. Mary recalled, "The guys were very involved and looked forward to our visits…of course a woman with round eyes in Vietnam always drew a lot of attention. The Army cooks helped make our refreshments and we loved the dog handlers, they were great guys."

Many soldiers wanted to do nothing more than talk; others to hear a soft voice, others to gaze upon a blonde-haired woman. Mary said, "Sooner or later they would ask us about our big canvas bags, 'Hey, what's in the bag today?' and within minutes we'd be conducting one of our programs." Red Cross recreation in a war zone required detailed planning. Mary recalled, "We'd call the fire support bases or LZs the night before. If they got hit in the mornings then we went there in the afternoons; if they're hit in the afternoons then we flew in that morning. I guess we were on a Viet Cong timetable. Explosions would still occur off base, usually land mines."

Mary never visited at a raid camp, fire support base, or LZ that received incoming during her visits. Qui Nhon, however, was a different story. Mary said, "The second week at Qui Nhon a unit leader ran in and said, 'We're on Red Alert, put on your flak vests, helmets, and pull a mattress over your heads. She walked out the door then we heard her yell, 'Oh, my God!' Light travels faster than sound, so she saw the ammo dump go up in a big ball of fire before the sound hit us. The shock wave moved the hooch walls to the end of their nails, then mortar rounds came in. After the alert one of our drivers told us he couldn't believe we were safe, that the mortar rounds danced all around our hooch but never hit us."

Her posting at Qui Nhon lasted five months. During another attack, their Red Cross recreation room took a direct hit; all the personnel had just left, nobody was hurt.

Mary's next port-of-call actually was a port, the enormous anchorage of Cam Ranh Bay. "Cam Ranh was very active," she recalled. "We had a nice rec center and went on missions to places like Tuy Hoa. Plus, we had new recruits coming in all the time. They couldn't believe the first thing they saw in Vietnam was round-eyed women, it made them feel good, boosted their morale. Those young boys thought 'maybe I will make it home.' By that time I had come to hate war."

Mary served her last three months of duty in the Mekong Delta. "My base was Binh Thuy," she said. "The Mekong Delta witnessed a lot of war but by 1971 most of our boys had gone home. My old roommate, Ilene, met up with me again in the Delta. One day we flew on a chopper near the Cambodian border. Well, Ilene and I had been to the village in that area before, but our chopper pilots were new and they flew right by a mountain that we recognized. We realized the chopper was in Cambodia. The pilots had been given the wrong coordinates. We got out of there real fast!"

On another mission Mary fell asleep in the chopper while the door gunners cleared their machine guns. She said, "I know that sounds a bit crazy trying to sleep with machine guns being cleared, but after you'd been in Vietnam for so long you just get used to it. However, a spent shell casing struck my leg and I thought I'd been hit. I nearly jumped out of my skin. Scared me to death!"

Her final thoughts on the Delta: "I know our soldiers hated the Delta but I loved it. By 1971 we were allowed to go off base into the local economy, to eat, to shop. We were on a boat once, minus one of the crewmembers because he was on leave. He came back a week later and was killed on the same boat. Yeah, the war still raged, but Ilene and I did more traveling in the Delta than anywhere else."

Her opinion of American soldiers and the Vietnamese: "We quickly learned that the military had all kinds of people, good guys, bad guys, ones that used drugs, others that drank, and boys that camped out in church. I came home with a lot of respect for the Vietnamese people who had to live in a country continuously at war. Most Americans haven't experienced such horror, gunfire around you every night, explosions, death all around you. I came to love the Vietnamese people; that year in Nam dictated the rest of my life."

Mary Atkinson Robeck continued to serve others. She helped Vietnamese boat people (refugees fleeing Vietnam in rickety vessels) by joining the Peace Corps in the West Indies. She recruited volunteers for the Peace Corps in Philadelphia, ended up in Indonesia and Singapore to process thousands of Vietnamese refugees for passage to the U.S., and taught English to help their transition. She met her future husband in Indonesia, a case worker; they flew home, got married, and flew back to Indonesia. Mary worked at a Boston Naval hospital for the Red Cross and another military hospital in Michigan, coordinated blood drives, served as a 2nd Lt in the National Guard, and finally had her two children at the age of 40 and 42.

"My husband and I have had a full, active life," she said. Asked if they enjoy retirement, Mary replied, "Shoot, we're not retired. I just took a new job with Habitat for Humanity as programs manager for the restores, accruing building supplies, bathtubs and sinks, things like that. My husband drives a school bus during the week and serves as emergency driver for a mental health center in Atlanta."

After a short pause, Mary reflected on Vietnam: "You know, when the guys left Vietnam they were happy. When I got on the plane coming home, I cried. I didn't want to leave, and I'd go back to do it again."

The words on the back of her Donut Dolly T-shirt: *A touch of home, in a combat zone; a smiling face, at a bleak firebase; the illusion of calm, in Vietnam.*

Rachel Torrance
The Bravest Women I Had Ever Met

Rachel on the right, crazy ass sailor in the middle.

Jack P. McCormick, chopper pilot: *"I would occasionally carry them out to the field to be with the troops when I was flying with the First Cav in 1970 out of Tay Ninh. These ladies were the bravest women I had ever met."*

While Jane Fonda was in North Vietnam aiding and abetting our enemy, women of character and selflessness served in Vietnam. Their mission was dangerous yet down-to-earth: Give our soldiers something to smile about, offer the boys a touch of home, and let the guys know they are respected and appreciated. These ladies were affectionately known as the Donut Dollies.

On April 12, 2015, one of these gracious ladies, Mrs. Mary Robeck, was featured in "A Veteran's Story." To my good fortune, another gracious lady, Rachel Torrance, surfaced in Monticello. This is her story.

"When I first came in-country I had to report to a commanding general and attend a dinner. I had no idea what I was doing," Rachel said. "At the dinner I sat beside his replacement, General Bond. Bond's wife was a Donut Dolly in WWII. Later in the war, General Bond became the only general in Vietnam killed by small arms fire. We always had dinner on Sunday evening with the general and his staff. It was strange, one evening we're mixing with the top echelon then the rest of the time we're together with enlisted guys and chopper pilots."

Vietnam is a long way from the farming community of Milledgeville, GA, the birthplace of Rachel Torrance. "We raised cotton, corn, soybeans; farm work is tough and your hands can get soiled, but that was nothing compared to the heat and grime of Vietnam." Rachel attended UGA after graduating from Baldwin County High School. "Coming back to the dorm one night I overheard a girl talking about Red Cross donut dollies. She had joined and that sparked my interest."

Rachel called and received an appointment with the Red Cross. "I took a Greyhound bus to Atlanta, then a taxi to a motel. The next day I went to the Red Cross southeast headquarters for a day long interview. One lady asked, 'Do you like men?' Well, I was too naïve to be scared, but I knew either a yes or no answer could work against me in diverse ways, so I told the truth. I replied, 'Well, I'm 22 years old, in college, grew up with three brothers…yes, ma'am, I like men.' She replied, 'That's damn good, because there's a lot of men in Vietnam!'"

Rachel was offered the job and accepted. "My father was okay with my decision then my mother surprised everybody with, 'No mother wants a child that far from home, but if you want to go you should.' A brother said, 'I can't advise you, I just volunteered for chopper training,' but my older sister thought I had lost my mind."

One thing Rachel recalled during her two week training in Washington, DC was the gamma globulin shot. "You knew when the girls received the gamma globulin injection," she said, smiling. "They were dragging one leg behind them." Rachel arrived in Saigon, Vietnam in

November, '69. "It was the middle of the night, machine guns all over the place, and the downtown hotel windows were taped. Pretty obvious we were in a war zone."

After additional training in Saigon, Rachel's first port-of-call was Long Bien. "We traveled mostly by chopper," she said. "A lot of girls stayed at Long Bien, but our hearts were at the fire support bases. We visited Xuan Loc often, but that was like a 4-H club compared to a fire support base. The fire support guys were humble, shy, even afraid to talk with us, sort of like, 'What are you doing here?', but after we'd initiated the conversation, the guys really warmed up, became very protective. The guys lived in primitive conditions, filthy all the time, but we loved them, great soldiers. You know, I grew up in farm country but never thought I was really dirty until Vietnam. We washed the grit from our hair every night, and I know your lady readers can appreciate that."

On one mission to Signal Mountain north of Saigon, Rachel was walking back to the chopper when she sensed a razor-sharp leg pain. A dog had left teeth marks in her flesh. (Dogs in Vietnam did not like the scent of perfume; they'd snarl and raise their hackles). Rachel cleaned the bite with a dirty rag found in the chopper. She received proper treatment at Long Bien but was confined to base for a series of 14 rabies shots into her stomach.

March of 1970: Rachel is transferred to Phuoc Vinh, north of Bien Hoa. "I was with the 1st Cav," she said. "I loved the Cav. Those boys were in dogged combat, fighting all the time, lots of fire support bases, a great bunch of guys. At a recent reunion, one of my friends reminded me of how we dodged the Grim Reaper at a 1st Cav fire support base named Flashing. No tree line, no real perimeter, and only one bunker used as the fire direction center. Instead of outgoing, we heard incoming. We were standing outside the bunker, startled, but one of the guys quickly pushed us into the bunker. It hit nearby."

"The base commander was flying in a Loach observation chopper above the camp and received the news that a couple of donut dollies were on the ground and under fire. He landed almost immediately and ordered the Loach crew to fly us out. I suppose it wouldn't have done his career much good losing two donut dollies. The guys formed a circle around the Loach, bare chested with no flak vests, cheering and protecting us. A couple boys picked up pieces of shrapnel to give us as souvenirs. As the chopper spiraled out we saw one chopper that had been destroyed and numerous shell craters. That's when we got scared, after the fact."

Donut dollies normally had to 'hitch' a ride to their destinations. When stuck at huge bases like Tan Son Nhut, the dollies would use the control tower's radio to send the message, 'Hey, donut dollies stranded at Tan Son Nhut, anybody going to Long Bien?' Rachel recalled, "That usually caused additional activity in the traffic pattern."

George Meeker, "Ghostrider" Helicopter crew chief: *"The Donut Dollies would visit Camp Holloway in the Central Highlands. It was a welcome touch of home from real American women."*

April and May of 1970: Rachel said, "Our unit director T.W., short for Tumbleweed because she was from Texas, kept a map to watch the movement of fire support bases. She was studying her map one day then suddenly said, 'Rachel, look at what's happening…we're crossing the border!' The invasion of Cambodia was underway. The soldiers were hyped-up, it was payback time, no more sanctuaries for the VC and NVA. I know the people back home were having hissy fits about the invasion but the guys were happy to finally accomplish something significant in the war. I never really figured out the war and being over there made things even cloudier."

Incoming was something to endure yet never get used to. Rachel said, "You know, after I returned to the States I was in bed one night when it thundered. I ended up on the floor." On being in an artillery pit: "If the guys received a support call we'd take a break and sit on the sandbags while they fired the big guns. It was neat then, but we paid for it later." Rachel has hearing loss, mostly low pitch sounds. She's worn hearing aids for years.

Rachel was given an opportunity to work at Camp Eagle with the 101st Airborne. She said, "I casually accepted, didn't show any excitement." Underneath her casual demeanor, Rachel was doing backflips. One of her brothers, Richard, flew choppers for the 101st. "I was in the mess hall when the field director said, 'Rachel, a soul brother called wanting your phone number to wish you a happy birthday but I wouldn't give it to him.' I replied, 'You jackass, that's my real brother and it really was my birthday!' Richard told the folks back home he was flying a desk, in no danger. He'd already been shot down once and his copilot seriously injured."

She recalls walking to the officers club with Richard. "Two jeeps loaded down with girls passed us on the way to a stand down. Even in that big open area the fragrance of perfume was very distinct. I couldn't believe my brother, he was sniffing the air like an old hound dog. That was so funny."

Rules were made; rules were broken. "I pulled a real coup being at the same base with my brother. And, yes, at fire support bases we shared a beer or two with the guys. If offered a beer, we'd say, 'You don't have anything else, do you?' But if offered a different beverage, we'd again state, 'You don't have anything but beer, right?' The boys caught on real fast."

No 'going away' parties for Rachel. With just a couple days left 'in-country' a typhoon cut her tour short. "I had to get my act together and get out of there quick, but those were some of the best days of my life. I think we all knew it would be an important year in our life, but didn't realize it would affect us for the rest of our lives."

Her worse day: "Some guys from the 101st got stuck in the rain for days on end, no food, no ammo, no way to get them out. They finally made it in, but with bleeding feet and bleeding hands from just being wet for so long. I saw a lot of things in Vietnam, but for some reason that stuck with me."

Her best day: "Every day. Yes, a lot of horror, but we visited hospitals and the guys appreciated us being there. We went out to a river barge manned by a bunch of Navy guys, very competitive men, we really had a great time with them. I know the Vietnam War was divisive at home, but we were there to help the guys that fought that war, to make them smile, to give them hope...yes, we did our part."

After returning home, Rachel Torrance spent over 30 years with UGA'S extension service. Since 2001 she's stayed busy with volunteer work in the community and leadership development. She sits on the housing authority board, tax equalization board, and the historical foundation board.

In the late 1990's, Rachel returned to Vietnam with several veterans to participate in a journey from Saigon to Hanoi. She scaled a mountain in Laos, part of the infamous Lam Son 719 battle in early 1971. Avoiding unexploded munitions during their climb, Rachel let the men take the lead. Smiling, she stated, "There I was surrounded by men in Vietnam, just like in the good old days."

Camillia Meyerson

Glenn Carr, Executive Officer of the 213th Chinook Helicopter Company at Phu Loi. *"I recall a Donut Dolly named Camilla, flew her to several locations in Vietnam. Thirty five years later a Donut Dolly, our first one, joined the Atlanta Vietnam Veterans Business Association. Her name is Camilla Meyerson. You guessed it...thirty five years after the war, we met again."*

Celebrating Rosie

Carol Cain as Rosie the Riveter

More than 10 million women of all races, creeds, and colors joined the workforce during WWII to replace the males who were destined for the battlefields. These enthusiastic ladies, affectionately known as 'Rosie the Riveters', filled a variety of jobs building warships, tanks, guns, aircraft, ammunition, plus thousands of other critical duties. "We Can Do It,' on the iconic WWII Rosie the Riveter poster became their battle cry.

Twelve Rosie the Riveters and 13 male WWII veterans were honored in November at the Benning Club at Ft. Benning, GA as part of the WWII Rosie the Riveter Social. Over 250 folks were in attendance, sponsored by the American Rosie the Riveter Association. Entertainment was presented by the talented Carol Cain from LaGrange who performed her remarkable Rosie the Riveter one-lady show, plus a cameo appearance by President Franklin D. Roosevelt (reenactor and Vietnam veteran, Dr. Hal Raper, Jr.). The few honorees I had the pleasure to interview were archetypical of the Greatest Generation, hard-working, no nonsense, patriotic Americans.

Elizabeth Minton of Pine Mountain Valley, GA worked as a riveter in Torrance, CA. She recalled, "We made bomb bay doors for the A-26 Invaders. The A-26 started out as a light bomber in Europe. It was mothballed after the war, flew again in the Korean War, mothballed a second time then flew combat in Vietnam. The Invader was a beautiful aircraft." During WWII, Elizabeth earned two E pins for 'excellence' in production.

When asked about the '4,000' hour patch stitched on her Rosie outfit, Elizabeth explained, "My husband, Ray, and I worked at the Little White House in Warm Springs for 13 years, putting in over 4,000 hours. Ray also served in WWII, including the battle for Iwo Jima. His unit carried supplies to the front lines. At night his unit picked up shrapnel off the runways. They used big lights for illumination. Ray said the hair on the back of his neck would stand up because they knew enemy snipers had them in their sights. Thank goodness he made it home."

Later in the war, Elizabeth made parts for the P-80 fighter, America's first combat jet. A family friend of the Mintons, Thomas Ferebee, visited their home often. Ferebee was the bombardier who released the atomic bomb from the B-29 Enola Gay over the Japanese city of Hiroshima. Regarding her longevity, Elizabeth stated, "God's not ready for me. I have my ticket, but I'm not ready to use it yet."

Riveter June Tinker built and repaired the B-25s and B-29s at Patterson Field just outside of Dayton, OH. "I was 17 years old," she said proudly. "I thought it was great having a paying job. Back then money was tight but we also wanted to do our part to win the war. I quit school in the eleventh grade thinking I'd go back to school after the war. Instead, I got married." At age 40, June earned her GED at Fort Benning, joined the civil service, and worked in food services until she retired. Her two brothers joined the Marines; one lost his life on Iwo Jima. She recently wrote a song "Gold Star Mother" telling the story of a mother losing her son to war.

Colonel Joe Bell was in attendance. Colonel Bell served in the Army Air Corps in WWII, received the Purple Heart in Korea, and served as an FO (forward observer) in Vietnam. Alzheimer's has dampened his memory, but not enough to fog his remembrance of Vietnam. "My team covered all the firebases," he said proudly. Colonel Bell sported a huge grin when I said, "*Welcome home, Colonel.*"

Fay Edwards certainly did her part during the war. She made piston rings for the Arm and Hammer Piston Ring Company in Baltimore, MD before joining the WACs in 1944. As a WAC, she saw service in France and Germany.

Eva Ulrich replied, "I'm afraid so," when asked if she too was a Rosie the Riveter. A genuine groundbreaker, Eva was one of the first women assigned to Lawson Field at Fort Benning in 1941. "There were six of us," she said. "I graduated from college in 1941 so I ended up as a base accountant. And, no, I didn't cook the books. Then one day I'm at the

Eight-Thirty Club in Columbus when this guy saunters up and asked me to marry him. Can you imagine that?" Asked her response, Eva said, "I said, yes, of course!" The impromptu romance lasted for 48 wonderful years.

Vincent Melillo, at age 97, is the only remaining member of the famous Merrill's Marauders living in Georgia. Vincent joined the Army in 1940, served in the West Indies and Panama, then volunteered with buddies for 'a dangerous mission.' He recalled, "We returned to the States for a short stint then traveled to California, and in short order found ourselves in the China, Burma, India theatre of operations. In nine months we walked over 1,000 miles through the nearly impenetrable jungles of Burma and India. Seven of those nine months were behind Japanese lines." Vincent also saw combat in Korea.

Luther Wise survived 30 missions over Europe as a B-17 tail gunner. A proud veteran of the celebrated 8th Air Force, Luther recalled one mission to Berlin with rousing hilarity. "Well, our radio operator had, let's say, an upset stomach. He really had to go and there were no bathrooms on a B-17, so a combat helmet had to do. Our fully loaded bomb bay served as a disposal site. Yep, on that mission we literally bombed the crap out of Berlin."

Doctor Fran Carter was one of 14,000 employees at the Bechtel-McCone-Parsons aircraft plant in Birmingham, AL. "I was a riveter on the B-29s," she said. "I showed my husband, John, a piece of defective workmanship before he entered the military. He said, 'That settles it, I'm not staying inside an airplane!' He volunteered for airborne so he could get out of airplanes as fast as possible." John participated in Operation Dragoon, the Invasion of Southern France.

She continued, "I'd been teaching school but every boy I dated went into the service so I decided to do my part, plus the sixty cents an hour doubled my teaching salary. I liked working as a riveter. When the war finally ended, John took advantage of the G.I. Bill so we both attended the University of Illinois. After receiving our doctorate degrees we taught at Samford University. You know, when we entered the University of Illinois our son was only 14 months old, but somehow that little boy still grew up to be normal." That 'little boy' retired from the military as a Lt. Colonel.

Rosie the Riverter Convention—Ft Benning, GA

Mabel Myrick worked as a colonel's executive secretary at the Pentagon. She said, "I took dictation from the colonel, processed interoffice memos and all the letters we mailed out." She often took the correspondence to Secretary of War Stimson for his personal signature. When asked her opinion of the Pentagon, Mabel replied, "It was BIG!"

The Greatest Generation, America will never see their like again.

Known But To Their Countrymen

Female warriors attained respect and everlasting glory for their battlefield feats throughout history, but most remain unknown to contemporary civilization due to a lack of interest in world history or kowtowing to mind-numbing political correctness. Many isolated regions of mother earth teach their history via word of mouth, legends, or homegrown folklore, while others produce meticulous documents, unless revised, to prove the existence of their national heroines.

The Vietnamese 'Joan Of Arc'
"Her Breasts Were Three Feet Long."

The first thing I noticed after setting my combat boots 'on the ground' in Vietnam, was the heat. It hit my face like the heat from a pot belly stove when you open the top door to add more wood to a blazing fire. It's a dry heat, a choking heat, and your lungs are advising you to 'go home'. To feel what I felt, close all your car windows on a hot summer day then turn the heater on full blast, close the door and wait outside for about three minutes. Then reopen the car door, scoot inside, close the door, and put your face in front of a heater vent and leave it there for 12 months. Welcome to Vietnam.

You'd think that rain would help. Nada, and keep in mind the water gushing from the sky in Vietnam is not called rain; rather, it's identified as a monsoon. Rain normally cools; a monsoon doesn't cool, it irritates. When a monsoon takes a pause during its season, the air transforms into a sticky humidity magnet, saturating your fatigues with salty sweat which saturates your skin which ripens into jungle rot. And your over-worked lungs are still advising you to 'go home'.

Consequently, you're fighting an invisible foe while coping with soggy fatigues, jungle rot, and overworked lungs in a foreign land where all the indigenous look the same. The natives who all look the same are even advising you to 'go home'. Considering the unreasonable rules of engagement laid upon us by wily politicians in air-conditioned basement war rooms at 1600 Pennsylvania Avenue, we should have 'gone home'. My brothers and sisters were in a country that had been dominated by foreign powers for thousands of years. America's involvement in Southeast Asia was a meager ten thousand day blip on the radar screen of Vietnam's struggle to be Vietnam. And Vietnam's nemesis for thousands of years was not France nor Japan nor the United States; their archenemy was to the north: China.

Trieu Thi Thrin
'Her voice was crystal clear and rang like a temple bell. She stood nine feet tall and her breasts were three feet long.'

Most Asian historians support the voice fable, but the latter two attributes have come into serious question. Her name was Trieu Thi Thrin, the 'Vietnamese Joan of Arc'.

Approximately 1200 years before Joan of Arc said her first prayer and picked up her first sword, Trieu Thi Thrin led a rebellion in the 3rd century against those pesky Chinese invaders from the north. With an army of approximately 1,000, she kept the Chinese occupiers at bay. Donned in elegant bright yellow robes called a quan aos, Trieu led her troops into combat sitting atop a war elephant while brandishing two unique swords. She liberated vast territory yet eventually lost the war. Legend claims she committed suicide after her defeat at the age of 23.

One of Trieu Thi Thrin's quotes is befitting the women's rights movement of the 21st century: *"I'd like to ride storms, kill sharks in the open sea, drive out aggressors, reconquer the country, undo the ties of serfdom, and never bend my back to be the concubine of a man."*

A Female Strategist And A Female Assassin At The Wadi Kishon

In 1125 B.C., Deborah, an Israeli judge, oracle, and military strategist, teamed up with Jael, a tent-dwelling tinsmith and practitioner of the first Israeli battlefield lobotomy, to win a decisive victory against the powerful Canaanite army at the Wadi Kishon.

In Hebrew, Deborah means 'bee', but also carries the meaning, 'a fiery or spirited woman', while Jael means 'wild goat' or 'wild gazelle'. The 'bee' planned the battle; the 'wild gazelle' ended it. Both women are acknowledged as national heroines by the Israeli nation. The commander of the Israelis, Barak, with fewer soldiers and lighter weapons, realized his prospects for victory were slim to none. Sisera, the Canaanite commander, vastly outnumbered the puny Israeli forces and possessed what was then considered weapons of mass destruction: iron armaments and 900 iron-rimmed chariots. Sisera was confident of victory, over-confident.

Deborah was not a 'judge' in modern-terms. Her duties as a 'judge' in the B.C. epoch meant during peacetime she had the authority to solve social problems and settle disputes. If war came, a 'judge' became the local 'recruiter' and called for the tribes to bear arms plus assisted in organizing the battle strategy and/or resistance. As an oracle, Deborah sat in her courthouse (actually under a particular palm tree in the hill country of Ephraim) then listened to a tribal complaint or problem before offering words of advice.

A contradiction does exist concerning the Israeli response to Sisera and the Canaanites. Deborah's territory around Ephraim was in disarray, law and order had broken down, and passage along the main roads was no longer safe. Albeit, the culprits of this mess were largely the doings of Israelite settlers in the hill country of Canaan who constantly raided Canaanite hamlets and homesteads. Sort of reminds one of the present day hissy-fits in the Golan Heights, the West Bank, and the Gaza Strip. To pick sides in the long history of Israeli/Arab hostility, one must realize this cultural and religious bickering has existed for thousands of years, so good luck picking sides. Personally, I'm holding out for Armageddon. But I digress. The Canaanite solution to the Israeli problem was complete extermination of the Jews, the equivalent extermination strategy advocated by Israel's present-day enemies, which leaves little room for compromise.

To cut a long story short, Deborah calls for an audience with Barak, the Israeli commander. I venture their conversation went something like this:

Deborah: "We have problem. You need to stop and defeat Sisera."

Barak: "Ma'am, he vastly outnumbers my weaker force. He has iron-rimmed chariots and iron weapons. We have bows and arrows and a few sling-shots."

Deborah: "And your point is?"

Barak: "Ma'am, my point is, we can't win."

Deborah: "Go to Mount Tabor with your army and I'll draw Sisera into a trap."

Barak: "Do what?" (Barak was born and raised in southern regions).

Deborah: "Do exactly as I say and have faith in God."

Barak: "Yeah, right."

Apparently Barak found faith in God or Deborah or both. He assembled his motley crew of citizen soldiers atop Mount Tabor and awaited Sisera's seemingly unstoppable army. Apparently Deborah understood a subject Barak and Sisera had little knowledge of: the weather. A downpour turned the rock-hard battlefield into a Milton Literary Festival mud-hole and a flash flood swelled the Wadi Kishon into a lake run amuck. The inundated ground added to the agony of iron-rimmed chariots trying to maneuver in mud. The chariots bogged down, they were stuck, with no place to go, rats in a barrel, and made easy targets for Israeli bows and arrows and a few sling-shots. The luckless Canaanites were slaughtered.

Sisera tucked tail and skedaddled from the battle. He was defeated, disgraced, and ran towards the encampment of a confederate, Heber, who often outfitted Sisera's army with weapons. Heber's wife, Jael, crafted oodles of weapons for the Canaanites, but unknown to Sisera, Heber's spouse had strong kinship ties to the Israelis. When Sisera finally made it to Heber's encampment, dehydrated and dog-tired, Jael invited him into her tent.

Now, here's the kicker. There were firm rules of hospitality in ancient Middle East. An invited guest was to be cared for, accepted, and protected; no excuses allowed. But unfortunately a slight snag existed for Sisera; only males could offer the compulsory hospitality to strangers. Jael was not obligated to care for nor protect Sisera. A Canaanite insect had entered an Israeli web.

Sisera was parched. Jael provided goat milk to quench his thirst. Sisera was tired and afraid. Jael covered him with a rug. Sisera fell asleep. According to Hebrew Scriptures in Judges 4: 21-24, this then transpired: *"She put her hand to a tent peg, and her right hand to the worker's mallet; She struck Sisera a blow, She crushed his head, She shattered and pierced his temple. He sank, he fell; he lay still at her feet, dead."*

After Jael implemented the first Israeli battlefield lobotomy, she scurried outside to greet Barak, who had come in search of Sisera. Several versions in dissimilar Holy Bibles hint at Jael's spoken words, but again I venture their conversation went something like this:

Jael: "The dude you're looking for is inside my tent."

Barak: "Is he armed?"

Jael: "Well, if he has returned from the dead and pulled the tent peg out of his brain, yeah, I suppose you could say he's armed with a tent peg."

Barak: "Do what?"

End of story.

The Chinese Prostitute Turned Pirate

The well-documented history of 'Pirate Queen' Ching Shih is a journal of survival, shrewdness, intelligence, and very few morals. Ching Shih commanded over 300 ships and an army of 30,000 soldiers during the 18th and 19th centuries. She was born Shin Yang in 1775. As a young woman, Shin made a living as a Cantonese prostitute and as the madam of a floating brothel. Judge her not too harshly. Chinese women in those days had few employment opportunities, as did most women. But I digress.

Anyway, in 1801 Shin Yang married an infamous pirate named Cheng I and became his partner in crime. When Cheng I died in 1807 at the age of 39, ironically in Vietnam, Shin Yang, now known as Ching Shih, consolidated her power and wealth by seducing her stepson, Cheung Po. Perhaps the precursor of organized crime, a Chinese Lucky Luciano if you will, Ching Shih laid down and enforced a strict code of 'pirate laws'. Her Pirate Code, in simple terms:

1. Violate the Pirate Code and lose your head.
2. Never steal from friendly villages.
3. All ill-gotten gains are to be shared.
4. Actual money is turned over to the squadron commander who will divvy up a certain percentage to his men but the majority of money goes to maintain the fleet and purchase provisions.

If one of her pirates raped a female captive, he lost his head. If the sex was consensual, the pirate lost his noggin, and the female, well, her legs were chained and weighed down with cannon balls. Then she was tossed overboard.

Ching Shih and her stepson-lover ran havoc as pirates until January of 1810. Cornered and defeated in the Naval Battle of Chek Lap Kok by the Portuguese Navy, they and their band of pirates would certainly face harsh treatment. Uh, not exactly.

Ching Shih and Cheung Po were granted amnesty by the Quin Imperial Government and the Governor of Guangdong Zhang Bailing dissolved their mother and son relationship so they could marry. Of the 17,318 pirates, only 126 were executed. Twelve years after their surrender, Cheung Po died at sea and Ching Shih decided to relocate her family to Macau.

In Macau, Ching Shih returned to her old tricks (pardon the pun). She launched a brothel and gambling house, plus dabbled in the salt trade. Later, while in her early 60's, she served as a Chinese military advisor against the British Empire during the first Opium War. The prostitute, madam, stepson-seducing swashbuckler, wheeler and dealer and salt trader, died in 1844 in Macau, with a rather large family surrounding her bedside. She was 69 years old.

Calico Jack's Two Ladies

The British pirate John Rackman, better known down in the Caribbean as 'Calico Jack' due to his habit of wearing calico garb, had two ladies aboard his ship, Anna Bonny and Mary Read. Mary dressed as a man. Anna didn't need to cross-dress; she was Calico Jack's lover and bore him a child. In 1720, their ship was attacked by a Royal Fleet. Being expert swordsmen, Anna and Mary fought against the British ships and sailors with the help of only one crewman. The other pirates were below deck, inebriated and hiding in fear. Captured and brought to trail, both women claimed to be with child and received a stay of verdict. Mary did give birth but died from complications. No records exist of Anna's fate. Fancy dresser Calico Jack had his neck stretched. As an interesting side note, Calico Jack's first mate, a pirate named Karl Starling, designed the Jolly Roger flag of a skull and cross swords, now famously represented as a skull and cross bones.

The Dahomey Amazons

An all-female military regiment called the Dahomey Amazons, served and fought for the African kingdom of Dahomey (1600-1894), now a territory of present day Benin. Dahomey lady warriors were named 'Amazons' by Western historians and observers due to their similarity to the semi-mythical Amazons of the Black Sea and antediluvian Anatolia. An 'Amazon' could volunteer for duty or be 'volunteered' for service, some as young as eight years old. They were physically powerful, well-trained, unafraid in combat, forbidden to marry, and were known for the substantial number of virgins within their ranks. When European encroachment unsurprisingly led to conflict, the Dahomey male warriors and female Dahomey Amazons fought two significant wars against the French. In the second war, the Dahomey fighters were decisively defeated by the better-armed French during the Battle of Adegon on October 6, 1890. Several French casualties were the result of French soldiers hesitating to bayonet the lady Amazons. Even so, it was a massacre. Male Dahomey KIA—86. Amazon KIA—417. The French lost six soldiers. Disbanded, the shrewd and vengeful Amazons who survived the slaughter formed a covert corps with only one goal: to assassinate French officers. The last known Amazon was a woman named Nawi. Nawi died in 1979, well over 100 years in age.

The Lady Wasn't Properly Equipped

During a routine medical examination of Spanish marines in 1798, the examiners observed that a Marine named Antonio lacked the compulsory paraphernalia to be classified as a man. Antonio did, however, expose soft parts that qualify her as a woman. Antonio's real name was Ana Maria de Soto. She was the first 'infante de Marina' (female Marine) in the world. Posing as a male in 1793, Ana joined the Spanish Armada and went to war on the frigate *Mercedes*. She was 16 years old. Ana fought in numerous battles. Ironically, when discovered as an 18th century cross-dresser, and instead of being ridiculed or booted off the ship, Ana (Antonio) received a promotion to sergeant and was granted the same pay as a man. When she intermittently wore women's clothing, Antonio Ana Maria de Soto was authorized to display her sergeant's chevrons and the marines' colors on her clothing.

The Fighting Nun

A century before Antonio-Ana donned men's clothing, another Spanish female from the Basque Country rejected her family's insistence on her career as a nun. At fifteen years of age, Catalina de Erauso would have nun of it (excuse my play on words). She disguised herself as a man, took the name Francisco de Loyola, split the convent on March 18, 1600 and sailed to the New World. Francisco/Catalina (take your pick) fought in countless battles. Captured and made a prisoner, she confessed her duplicity to a bishop who persuaded her to reenter a convent. But as her legend spread across The Pond, the archbishop of Lima requested her presence. The year was 1620. Apparently Catalina de Erauso de la Fancisco de Loyala—or whoever—took her leisurely time: she arrived in Spain four years later, in 1624, having fought in yet another battle after which she was obliged to change ships. Two years later on June 29, 1626, she was given an audience with Pope Urban VIII. It seems that Pope Urban aspired recognition as the first progressive liberal pontiff: He granted Catalina de Erauso a special dispensation allowing her to wear men's clothing.

Who Really Killed Golden Hair?

Faulty Intelligence. It's a killer. Such was the case at the Battle of Little Big Horn, also recognized as Custer's Last Stand, or from a Native American Indian point of view, the Battle of the Greasy Grass. Imaginably, the fight should have been called Last Stand on the Bloody Grass. The date was June 25, 1876.

Lt. Col. George Armstrong Custer, nicknamed Golden Hair, not by Native Americans but by Hollywood, actually had several real nicknames: Autie, The Boy General, and Ringlets, due to his long curly blonde hair, although by the time Little Big Horn entered the history books his hair was thinning, so much so that Custer and only one other soldier escaped scalping. The soldiers of the 7th Cavalry Regiment, however, referred to Custer as Iron Butt or Hard Ass.

Well, old Iron Butt believed he was up against no more than 300-400 Indian warriors. Faulty Intelligence, it's a killer. The Arapaho, Sioux, and Northern Cheyenne encampment bristled with between 1500 to 4000 Indian braves, or thereabouts. The number discrepancy in warriors is not the only issue debated regarding the battle at Little Big Horn, including who delivered the fatal blow to old Iron Butt. Custer's five companies were annihilated to the last man, consequently, historians have developed their conclusions based on Native American myths, legends, and by word of mouth passed down via each tribe for over a century.

It is known, however, that a squaw named Buffalo Calf Road Woman, fought in combat alongside her husband, Black Coyote. She rode into the battle to save the life of her brother, one of the paramount acts of courage in the violent engagement. The Cheyenne also claim that Buffalo Calf Road Woman was the one who knocked Custer off his horse during the mêlée.

Another claim to Custer's demise comes from the Hunkpapa Sioux. A Sioux squaw named Moving Robe Woman, or Thasina Mani in her own language, yet also called Walking Blanket Woman, She Walks With Her Shawl, Mary Crawler, or Her Eagle Robe (identifying her given name must have played havoc at the local post office, but I digress) led one of the countercharges against Custer to avenge the battlefield killing of her brother, One Hawk. Her dad, Crawler, also participated in the battle. Now enters the Fog of War, or better yet, Faulty Intelligence. An Oglala Lakota Sioux, Fast Eagle, made the claim he held down Custer's arms as Moving Robe Woman stabbed old Iron Butt in his back. Nice fairytale. No stab wounds were reported on Custer, post mortem.

The Lady Samurai

Long before actor Tom Cruise played the part of a renegade American cavalry officer and Ken Watanabe portrayed the samurai general Katsumoto in the blockbuster film *"The Last Samurai"*, a female samurai fell in combat much like Katsumoto's demise in the movie. Incidentally, Facebook addicts spread a rumor that the Japanese were upset because Watanabe was of Chinese ancestry, not Japanese. More Facebook balderdash; Ken Watanabe is Japanese. Anyhow, the Land of the Rising Sun (Nippon or Nihon, carrying the same meaning), better known to the outside world as Japan, inventor of the fortune cookie…yes, that's correct, the fortune cookie was a Japanese invention, not a Chinese after-dinner treat, via San Francisco resident and Japanese confectionery owner, Mr. Suyeichi Okamura, in 1906. And that's not the last time I'm likely to digress, but let's move on.

Nakano Takeko is one of a very few recognized onna-bugeishas (female samurai) in the long, polygonal waring history of Japan. She excelled in martial and literary arts, instructed martial arts alongside her adopted father, and in 1868 led an ad hoc assemblage of female warriors who fought as an independent corps in the Battle of Aizu during the Boshin War, one of many Japanese civil wars. In combat she preferred using a naginta, meaning pole arm. While leading a charge against the Imperial Japanese Army, just like Katsumoto in 'The Last Samurai', a lethal bullet pierced her chest. Knowing the enemy would debase her body and take her head as a ghoulish war trophy, Nakano asked her sister, Yuko, to cut off her head then bury it. This, Yuko did. She buried her sister's head under a pine tree at the Hokai-ji Temple in what is now called Fukushima. Japanese women and adolescent girls honor Nakano Takeko yearly during the Aizu Autumn Festival. In spite of this, as revered as Nakano Takeko may be, she is not the most famous onna-bugeisha.

Tomeo Gozen

Approximately 700 years before Nakano Takeko held a sword or gripped a naginta, another woman named Tomoe was destined to be remembered as the most famous of female Samurai. She was called Tomeo Gozen, Gozen being a title of esteem bestowed upon her by her shogun Minamoto no Yoshinaka. She fought alongside male Samurai in the five year Genpei War from 1180 to 1185 and was acknowledged as an expert swordswoman and archer. Historians describe Tomeo as daring, well-liked, and knockout gorgeous.

Tomeo loved to mount wild horses then nudge them down steep slopes and had no qualms leading male Samurai into combat and conquest. Yet, when shogun Minamoto no Yoshinaka was killed in the Battle of Awazu, Tomeo hung up her bow and arrows and swords and presumably retired. She later married, but after her husband died, legend has it she became a nun.

Fascinating. So far we've discussed a Spanish woman who rejected her scapular and habit for a warrior's existence and a Japanese female who rejected her soldier's life for the coif and veil of a nun. Nun of this makes any sense (forgive me). Let's move on to Great Britain.

Queen Boudicca

Find a murder of Jackdaws (a band of Crows), jump on the back of the largest one then soar in a straight line from Nakano Takeko's Japan to jolly old England. As the Jackdaw flies, your trip will cover approximately 9,565 miles, but if you're skittish about depending on the dead reckoning of a Jackdaw, then travel by land and sea, a distance of about 13,334 miles.

Ah, yes, jolly old England in the good old days. Surviving in the Stone Age until the Neolithic Era evolved the future empire from foraging to farming, and large stones called henges dotted the landscape, as in Stonehenge, the dissimilar nomadic tribes of Celtic origin were known as Britons. That is, until my Italian ancestors came calling on August 26, 55 B.C. to conquer and control the Britons. After a few years of death and destruction, the land became known as Roman Britain, then Britannia, and later Britanniae, meaning The Britains.

King Prasutagus of a Celtic tribe called the Iceni, eventually allied with the Romans but demanded in his will that his daughters, alongside the Roman emperor, rule his kingdom as equals. Rome granted the right to inherit to males only, preferably a son. Consequently, when Prasutagus croaked, my ancestors invaded his dominion to kick butt and take names, plus raped his daughters and tortured his wife. Her name was Boudicca.

Suffice to say, Queen Boudicca was, as uttered in present-day unrefined lingo, pissed. In 60 A.D. or thereabouts, Boudicca called upon numerous Celtic tribes to unite and push the Romans back where they came from. Hell hath no fury as a raped queen. With approximately 100,000 troops under her command, Boudicca cut a swathe through Camulodunum, the Roman Capitol of Britain, now known as Colchester. And Queen Boudicca kept on cutting swathes. She seized Londinium (London) and Verulamium (St. Albans), leaving destruction in her wake and around 75,000 butchered souls.

Roman Emperor Nero, you know the dude, the pyromaniac fiddle-playing simpleton who fiddled while Rome burned, mulled over the idea of pulling completely out of Britain. Yet as Nero fiddled, the Roman Army ultimately defeated Boudicca's military, thus saving the fiddle-player from ordering an 'honorable withdrawal' and conceivably freeing up the arsonist to keep on fiddling.

What became of Queen Boudicca is unknown. She was not captured nor killed, therefore historians speculate Boudicca died by her own hand or sickness. A bronze statue of Boudicca riding a chariot into battle with her daughters by her side was erected at Westminster Bridge's western side in 1902. The base of the statue reads: *Boudicca, Queen of the Iceni, who died in AD 61 after leading her people against the Roman invader.*

Grace O'Malley

"Gran' me lads, nigh let's cross de Oirish sea from Liverpool to Dublin ter discuss a lady Oirish pirate."

Irish brogue translation: "Okay, my friends, now let's cross the Irish Sea from Liverpool to Dublin to discuss a lady Irish pirate."

Ireland in the 16th century, her name: Grace O'Malley, a female warrior and seafaring pirate. Young Grace wanted to set sail with her father, but momma said, "Naw, young lady, yer stayin' on land, yisser 'air 'ill be caught in de ropes." Grace solved the problem of 'your long hair will be caught in the ropes' by cutting off her locks and setting sail with a new nickname "Bald".

After her father kicked the bucket, Grace became chieftain of the O'Maille clan and ruled over the Umaill kingdom. Grace used the ships she inherited as pirate vessels for pillaging. All other ships, near her own vessels or near the shores of her kingdom, became fair game. In the vein of most well-to-do pirates, Grace charged these hostage ships a 'safe passage tax', her Irish approach of selling gangster-style 'protection'. Refusal to shell out the demanded bounty resulted in the broadside of a sword up against one's skull, or on a bad hair day, a swift detachment of one's head. She gave birth to a child aboard ship; the following day Grace was back in action defending her ship and/or reaping the booty of victims to feed her kid.

A thorn in Grace's maritime side was the irksome Queen Elizabeth I who was in the midst of consolidating her royal power and wealth by crushing Irish chieftains. Grace wrote Queen Elizabeth a 'let's make a deal' letter demanding that Grace remain free to practice the art of piracy as long as the piracy was against England's enemies. With her head on the line, or more appropriately the chopping block, Grace met face to face with the aggressive Queen and managed to sweet-talk Elizabeth into releasing her son and brother from ransomed captivity, plus was granted a return of all properties confiscated by the Queen's forces.

Queen Elizabeth granted Grace the green light to 'fight in our dispute with all the world.' Elizabeth spoke no Irish and Grace spoke no English; the two women conversed in Latin. Cautiously appeased with the Queen's offer, Grace returned to her kingdom while Elizabeth began another pillage and plunder crusade against Irish chieftains, clearly breaking their agreement. Undeterred, Grace O'Malley renewed her lucrative piracy but also fought against the English until her death in Rockfleet Castle in the year 1603, the same year of Queen Elizabeth's passing.

The Wickedest Flying Witches

Calling a female pilot a 'flying witch' in avant-garde America would bring condemnation, censorship, and protesters trampling down the weeds in my front yard. So, stick with me on this: The flying '*Night Witches*' of WWII gained their nickname from an adversary, out of respect for their boldness and deadly sneak attacks. Moral of the story: never sell a female pilot short.

The conduit to 'flying witches' most likely began with Katherine Wright, sister of the Wright brothers. Katherine not only flew with her brothers but contributed as much vigor and knowledge to the first flight at Kitty Hawk as did her famous brothers.

Harriet Quimby was the first woman in America to become a licensed pilot. Nice start, but it would take the U.S. military 65 years to accept female pilots plus another 17 years before the females were allowed inside the cockpits of combat aircraft.

Chopper pilot Major Marie Rossi was the first American female pilot to lose her life in a combat role on March 1, 1991 near her home base in northern Saudi Arabia. She was 32 years old.

Ranked as the top female Air Force pilot in the 1990s, Lt. Col. Martha McSally was the first woman to fly a fighter aircraft on combat sorties. She also flew over 100 combat hours in an A-10 Warthog over Iraq in the mid-90s. Also worthy of mention is Major Nicole Malachowski, who in 2006 became the first female to be recruited by the U.S. Air Force Thunderbirds performance team.

But the 'wickedest flying witches'? Really? While sounding degrading and an inappropriate way to describe female aviators, German soldiers fighting on the Eastern Front during WWII would disagree with any criticism of their chauvinistic characterization. They dreaded yet respected the "Night Witches" of the Russian Air Force; the most publicized and recognized of the three units being the 588th Night Bomber Regiment.

'Nachthexen' – The Night Witches

The ladies of the 588th flew antiquated Polikarpov PO-2 biplanes, a slow noisy aircraft developed in the 1920s. No match in aerial combat against German Messerschmitt Bf-109s or Focke-Wulf Fw-190s, PO-2s were constructed of fabric pulled over a plywood frame. They had no radio, no parachute, and no guns. The women navigated with a stopwatch and map, and could only carry two small bombs.

So the ladies adapted. They flew only at night and at tree top level in formations of three to avoid German ground defenses. So noisy was a PO-2 that the women aviators would quickly gain altitude then cut their engines as they neared the target, glide in, drop their bombs, restart their engines and head for home. With engines cut and gliding over their target, the PO-2s made a whooshing noise the German soldiers described as 'like a witch's broomstick in the night', thus the term 'Nachthexen', German for Night Witches.

Born and raised in the Donetsk coal mining district of Ukraine, Nadezhda Popova was one of the most highly-decorated and nationally treasured aviators of the 588th. She had the childhood dreams of most young girls, acting and dancing and music. Then one fortuitous day everything changed. She caught the aviation bug after a small plane landed near her village. Fascinated, she signed up for glider school without her parent's permission and by the age of 16 had made her first solo flight and first parachute jump. By her 18th birthday, Nadezhda's skill earned her a slot as a flight instructor.

During the German invasion of Russia, her town was taken over by the Wehrmacht; her home converted into a feared Gestapo Police Station, her brother had perished at the front, and she saw civilians gunned down by strafing German planes. Nadezhda decided to go to war.

Rumored to have been the first female volunteer in the newly formed all-women air groups, Nadezhda described the combat in many foreign and Russian interviews. Paraphrasing a few: "Our planes were tossed around in strong winds. During winter you'd get frostbite looking out to spot your target, our feet would freeze in our boots, but we carried on. You focused on the target, guessing how you could get hit, and had no time for emotions. If you gave in to the elements you were shot down and burned alive. We didn't have parachutes." After returning from one mission, her all-female ground crew counted over 40 bullet holes in Nadezhda's flimsy aircraft.

Nadezhda described being caught in German searchlights after a deadly and challenging mission: "I was attempting to maneuver away from the searchlights when I saw them switch to another plane. German fighters came in and shot her down. That was only the first one. I saw a second plane go down, then a third ignite and fall to earth like a blazing torch. We lost a total of four planes that night, eight girls burned alive. It was a nightmare, my dear friends, we had slept in bunks together."

Female pilots of the 588th ranged from 17 to 26 years old. Several died without having received their first kiss from a young man. Others who survived missions used their navigation pencils as lip liners in hopes of receiving that first kiss.

Shot down on several missions, forced to land damaged planes on others, Nadezhda was never seriously injured. In July of 1942, she was shot down and crash-landed in the North Caucasus. Uninjured, she eventually found and hooked up with a retreating Russian infantry unit. She met another downed aviator, slightly wounded but amusing, a male named Semyon Kharlamov. They hit it off immediately. They arranged to meet again several times during the war and both became 'Heroes of the Soviet Union' in the same decree by Joseph Stalin. They reached Berlin together and carved both their names into the walls of the Reichstag. The couple married after the war and stayed together until Semyon's death in 1990. Their only son, as of this writing, is a general in the Belarussian Air Force.

The Night Witches' tactics so irked the German High Command that the promise was issued to award the coveted Iron Cross to German fighter pilots fortunate enough to shoot down a Night Witch. A David vs Goliath syndrome was not a factor. The top air speed of a PO-2 was 110 miles per hour, the same stall speed of German fighters; meaning, to line up for a shoot down, the German fighters could lose power then crash and burn. Another factor was altitude. The Night Witches flew at tree top level, so low an altitude that German fighters could plow earth if unable to pull up in time. The antiquated biplanes were highly maneuverable and were not burdened by the weight of powerful engines. In an odd twist of fate, the PO-2s vulnerabilities proved to be its useful assets.

Nadezhda obtained the rank of Lt. Colonel, returned to flight instructor duties after the war, and is remembered as one of the best pilots who flew into combat for the 588th all-female aviation group. She was also one of the luckiest: Nadezhda completed 852 combat sorties, including 18 in one night. She was not alone. A 588th pilot Rufina Gasheva flew 848 night missions and Natalva Meklin completed an amazing 980 night missions. Both survived the war.

As with all warriors, war generates memories and Nadezhda was certainly no exception. In a 2010 interview, she stated the following.

"I sometimes stare into a darkness and close my eyes. I can still imagine myself as a young girl, up there in my little bomber, and I say to myself, Nadia, how did you do it?"

Of approximately 314,000 United States Air Force personnel, 61,000 are female. The ladies continue to break barriers and fill positions traditionally reserved for only men. They have earned the opportunity, yet on the ground in hand-to-hand combat, the jury is still out. Women have the true grit, they can acquire the training, but pluck and preparation simply does not equate to brute force. Perhaps the key word is 'brute', and hand-to-hand combat is indeed a brutal business. It requires brute strength, so maybe close quarters fighting should remain the profession of brutes, pun intended.

Lt. Colonel Nadezhda Popova 'went west' in Moscow, Russia on July 8, 2013. She was 91 years old.

The Sweethearts Of Sweetwater

Margaret Oldenburg

On March 7, 1943, Margaret Oldenburg and her instructor were practicing spins in a PT-19 open cockpit trainer. Unfortunately, the spin became uncontrollable. Oldenburg nor her instructor were able to recover the aircraft and both lost their lives in the resulting fiery crash. Oldenburg was the first WASP (Women's Auxiliary Service Pilots—WASP is plural) to lose her life in an organization that would eventually go down in history as the first American females to fly military aircraft.

On March 21, 1943, Cornelia Fort was behind the controls of a BT-13, ferrying the aircraft with a group of male pilots. One of the male pilots, believing or at least pretending he was a 'Top Gun', started showing off and flew too close to Fort's aircraft. His landing gear hit the wing of her plane and broke off a big portion of it. Fort's plane went into a nose dive and crashed, killing Fort instantly. At Pearl Harbor on December 7, 1941, Fort had eluded Japanese attacking fighter planes while flying as a private pilot.

Mabel Virginia Rawlinson was towing a flying shooting target at Camp Davis, NC on July 19, 1943 so the men on the ground could practice shooting at airborne targets. Many times due to misunderstanding, the men on the ground fired at the airplanes and several WASP pilots received foot wounds. Rawlinson was behind the controls of A-24 and started experiencing technical issues. The instructor told her to return to base. On her final approach, Rawlinson's plane clipped the top of a pine tree, the plane nosed down, and crashed. The instructor was thrown free with minor injuries. Rawlinson, however, was trapped inside as flames engulfed the aircraft.

Marion Hanrahan, another WASP also stationed at Camp Davis, wrote an eyewitness report: "I knew Mabel very well. We were both scheduled to check out on night flight in the A-24. My time preceded hers, but she offered to go first because I hadn't had dinner yet. We were in the dining room and heard the siren that indicated a crash. We ran out onto the field. We saw the front of her plane engulfed in fire, and we could hear Mabel screaming. It was a nightmare."

A crash investigation revealed that the towing aircraft had been poorly maintained and the Army Air Corps was using the wrong octane fuel.

Gertrude Tompkins Silver was the only WASP listed as MIA (Missing in Action) during WWII. She departed Mines Field (now known as LAX) for Palm Springs on October 26, 1944. Silver was flying the hottest fighter aircraft of the day, the P-51D Mustang, bound for New Jersey. She and the Mustang were never heard from again.

Since the WASP were federal service employees, they did not qualify for military benefits. Therefore, the thirty eight WASP killed in accidents, eleven in training, twenty-seven on active duty missions, were sent home at family expense. More often than not, other WASP pooled their monies so the remains of their fallen sisters could be sent home. The American flag was not even allowed to be placed on the coffin, although Mabel Rawlinson's family draped her coffin with Old Glory.

How good were these lady pilots? Over 25,000 applied for WASP training, 1,830 were accepted, yet only 1,074 graduated from flight school. Many came from wealthy families or had husbands rich enough to foot their expensive pilot training. At a risk of sounding chauvinistic, a quick review of WWII WASP photos would lead one to believe each one was drop dead gorgeous.

The lady pilots of WWII began as the WAFS (Women's Auxiliary Flying Squadron). Recruits were restricted to ages 21 to 35, had to have a high school diploma, a commercial flying license, 500 hours of flight time, and cross-country flying experience. They earned $250 monthly but were required to purchase their own uniform, plus provide and pay for their room and board.

Another group was known as the WFTD (Women's Flying Training Detachment) under the experienced leadership of Jacqueline "Jackie"

Cochran, a professional and world-renowned aviatrix. After the war, Cochran was the first woman to break the sound barrier.

Cochran wanted a single unit to control the activity of women pilots. With the backing, and influence, of First Lady Eleanor Roosevelt, plus the rank and muscle of General Henry 'Hap' Arnold and General Roberts Olds, the WASP program merged the WAFS and the WFTD into one unified training and ferrying program in July of 1943. The theory behind the programs for female pilots was to 'free-up' male aviators for combat duty. WASP freed approximately 900 male pilots.

The first training class was conducted at Howard Hughes Field in Houston, TX. Cochran, disappointed with the school and training facilities, moved the WASP to Sweetwater, TX and used an airstrip known as Avenger Field. During the war, the WASP pulled duty at 122 airbases in the U.S., delivered 12,652 aircraft of 78 different types which amounted to around 75% to 80% of all ferrying missions.

Most of the female pilots were Caucasian. However, Hazel Ying Lee and Maggie Gee, both Chinese Americans, also qualified to be a WASP. Hazel Ying Lee was the last WASP to perish during the program. Ola Mildred Rexroat, a Native American Oglala Sioux from the Pine Ridge Indian Reservation in South Dakota, flew as a WASP, as did two Mexican Americans.

An African American applicant, Mildred Hemmans Carter, was turned down because of her race, in spite of obtaining at age 19 a Bachelor of Arts degree from Tuskegee Institute and retained an aviation certificate. She was also rejected by the Tuskegee Airman program. Carter was recognized retroactively as a WASP seventy years later and at age 90 took her last flight. No records exist of how many African American women made the final interview, but they were all disregarded. Female aviatrix 'Jackie' Cochran told one black applicant, Janet Harmon Bragg, that, "It's difficult enough fighting prejudice aimed at females without additionally battling race discrimination."

Considering the nation was still in the ugly grips of segregation, Co-chran may have had no other choice. WASP were belittled by many male pilots and in some cases sabotaged. The *New York Daily News, TIME,* and the *Washington Post* advocated for the WASP to be replaced by men. Journalist Drew Pearson of the *Washington Times Herald* accused General Arnold of being influenced by 'Jackie' Cochran's "feminine wiles."

One base commander at Camp Davis, a Major Stephenson, told the WASP that, 'both they and their planes were expendable.' In one crash, Cochran found sugar in the engine at a WASP crash site. A total of 14 confirmed events of improper maintenance on towing planes are a matter of record at Camp Davis as were many incidents of the wrong octane fuel being used. At some bases, 'objectionable' aircraft were given out to the WASP. The base commander at Love Field in Dallas was officially castigated for treating women unfairly. In the area of pay, as with debates that still rage today, WASP received two-thirds the paycheck of their male counterparts.

Initially, the age cap of 35 for lady pilots was tailored 'to avoid the irrationality of women when they enter and go through menopause.' The male-dominated military had determined the age of 40 was most likely when women entered menopause, so if the war lasted five years or longer the WASP would only then be on the brink of 'debilitating irrationality.' WASP were grounded during menstrual cycles by many base commanders, believing that the female pilots were 'less efficient' during that time of the month. Air brakes were applied to that type of mentality after flight records disavowed the asinine claim.

Military planes did not have proper facilities for women to use the bathroom, therefore when ferrying planes the WASP had to land to find a restroom. Grabbing a quick bite to eat could also prove difficult since many restaurants refused service to the WASP because the ladies were wearing pants.

Albeit, the WASP flew just about every aircraft in the military inventory, including a few exceptionally qualified women who flew and tested rocket-propelled and jet-propelled aircraft. If a new aircraft was difficult to fly, like the YP-59 and originally the prone-to-fire B-29, General Arnold would recruit WASP to fly the planes to 'embarrass' the men into strapping into a cockpit. Dorthea Johnson and Dora Doughtery Strother were chosen to fly a B-29 to Alamogordo, where the Atomic bomb was being developed. Large crowds at Alamogordo awaited the female aviators to see them land. After that flight, male pilots ceased grumbling when assigned training on the B-29s.

All legislation put before Congress during WWII to confer the WASP with military status were defeated, even with General Arnold's backing and positive testifying. With the war nearing its end, the WASP were disbanded in December of 1944. These courageous ladies aviators flew over 60 million miles, handled the controls of advanced fighters, heavy bombers, transported much needed cargo, and even simulated hazardous strafing missions. Most of the WASP records were sealed for 30 years after WWII ended. Historians and researchers and journalists poured over other classified films, records, and reports when they were finally released, but the WASP story was seldom told or reported until the late 1970's. One incident in 1976 really stirred up the WASP nest. The Air Force proudly announced they were accepting women in their flying program and made the claim, 'it's the first time that the Air Force has allowed women to fly their aircraft.'

Hell hath no fury as a WASP scorned. The remaining WASP lobbied Congress to be militarized and persuaded former Presidential candidate and Senator Barry Goldwater to help with their crusade. Goldwater had also ferried military aircraft during WWII. Goldwater was shocked by the prejudice in Congress. Before Goldwater's help, a bill was introduced as early as 1972. It was defeated. With Goldwater's persistence and that of Colonel Bruce Arnold, son of General Hap Arnold, the walls of prejudice started crumbling down.

The G.I. Bill Improvement Act of 1977 provided WASP with VA benefits. Former WASP were issued Honorable Discharges in 1979. Each WASP was awarded the World War Two Victory Medal in 1984, with many of the medals accepted by family members of deceased WASP. In 2009, WASP were inducted into the International Air and Space Hall of Fame at the San Diego Air and Space Museum. President Barrack Obama awarded the Congressional Gold Medal to the WASP on July 1, 2009.

As a Vietnam veteran who vividly remembers the treatment we Nam vets endured during and after that war, it saddens me to know members of the Greatest Generation were also shunned proper recognition for decades after their faithful service to the United States of America. And like Vietnam vets, the WASP fell victim to the political whims of Washington, DC. If anything has been learned by the historical neglect of specific veteran groups by wily politicians, the foremost lesson is the solid resilience of the American patriot, male and female.

Perhaps current history and social teachers need to research and teach a new generation of the loyalty and love of country that came with the territory as a gift, not something to endure or protest. As one WASP commented, "We were children of the Great Depression. It was root hog or die. You had to take care of yourself. Nobody owed us anything."

The battle continues. The Army has ruled twice that the 1977 legislation did not mandate the burial of a deceased WASP at Arlington National Cemetery. Perhaps the fine print disallows these women a final resting place at Arlington, and granted the burial space at Arlington is quickly disappearing, yet as of 2016 only WASP cremated remains can be interred at Arlington, but not a ground burial.

"You and more than 900 of your sisters have shown that you can fly wingtip to wingtip with your brothers. If ever there was any doubt in anyone's mind that women can become skilled pilots, the WASP have

dispelled that doubt. I want to stress how **valuable** *I believe the whole WASP program has been to our country. We know, that you can handle our latest fighters, our heaviest bombers; we know, that you are capable of ferrying, target towing, test flying, and the countless other activities which you have proved you can do. So, on this last graduation day, I salute you and all WASP. We of the Army Air Force are proud of you, we will never forget our debt to you."*

— Hap Arnold,
Commanding General, USAF,
to the last graduation of WASP
at Sweetwater, TX, 1944

Lady Warriors

March 23, 2003: An enemy ambush inflicts heavy casualties on an Army Company near Nasiriyanic, Iraq. Two female soldiers, Shoshana Johnson and Jessica Lynch are wounded and captured. Jessica Lynch would later receive heroic yet controversial media coverage. Another lady warrior, Pfc Lori Piestewa, was killed in the ambush. Piestewa became the first American female to perish in the Iraq War. A Hopi Indian from Arizona and mother of two small children, she is thought to be the first female Native American Indian to die as a soldier in the service of her country. Among several honors, Squaw Peak in Phoenix was renamed Piestewa Peak in remembrance.

To properly honor America's fallen female warriors would take a book as thick as *War and Peace*. Albeit, ladies have participated in America's conflicts since the Revolutionary War and thousands have paid the ultimate price. This is the story of just a few.

The Revolutionary War: Without detailed physicals, untold numbers of small-framed (and more significantly, fully-clothed) warriors accompanied their fathers, husbands, lovers, and brothers in the fight for America's independence. Women with the calloused hands and leathered faces of strenuous life on the frontier looked as tough and mean as the males, a feature which disguised softer physical attributes. Well-known female veterans were even awarded benefits, but deficient paperwork and unmarked graves hid an untold number of female fatalities. One recorded death, a Creole girl named Sally St. Clair, followed her lover into combat and fought by his side. She gave her life protecting his during the Battle of Savannah.

The War of 1812: History does not treat female contribution too kindly in this two and a half year war. Sloppy record keeping can be blamed as well as a growing class of upper crust citizens with little feedback from the lower class. Journals, or more commonly, diaries, kept by officers' wives and well-to-do socialites recorded their views of the war from both sides.

No doubt female participation took place on the American side, mainly as spies, but women were usually portrayed as dutiful wives supporting their gone-to-war husbands. As the Napoleonic Wars raged in Europe, the conflict in the Americas was pretty much a sideshow, at least in British rationale. The Americans, however, felt the heat of the war when the British burned the Capitol in Washington, DC to the ground and the city of Detroit surrendered without one shot being fired.

Many American women followed their men camp to camp. If they lost a husband to war, the widows were given three to six months to grieve then had to remarry within the camp or vamoose. At least three official reports indicated widows who were married four times within five years. At sea, aboard the USS Constitution, Marine sharpshooter George Baker took a heavy toll on the British with his deadly aim in several major battles. Thing is, George Baker was actually Lucy Brewer. After the war, Lucy was finally acknowledged as the first female Leatherneck to serve her country. Having been deceived once, it would be over 100 years before the US Marines seriously recruited women.

The Mexican-American War: Considering the horrible fact that hundreds of American soldiers were buried in mass or unmarked graves during the Mexican campaign, one can imagine if a female was among them she will never be recognized.

Nonetheless, two females, a Mrs. Foley and a Mrs. Sarah Borginis enlisted with their husbands in the 8th Calvary at Jefferson Barracks in Missouri. Sarah became the head cook at Ft. Brown in Texas and remained on the job when General Zachary Taylor moved his forces to the mouth of the Rio Grande. When the Mexicans bombarded Ft. Brown, she was issued a musket and took an active part in the fight, allegedly never missing a shot or preparing a meal. General Taylor breveted her to Colonel, the first female Colonel of the US Army, albeit a brevet one. Sarah died in 1866 and was buried with full military honors at Ft. Yuma.

The American Civil War: Over 60 women were either killed or wounded during the conflict. One female from Michigan, a 19 year old known only as Emily, ran away from home to serve in the drum corps. She was fatally wounded in the battle for Chattanooga. As she lay dying, Emily dictated a letter to her father, "Please forgive your dying daughter. I have but a moment to live. My native soil drinks my blood; I expected to deliver my country but fate would not have it. I am content to die. Pray forgive me … Emily."

The bodies of two uniformed Confederate womenfolk were discovered after the Battle of Gettysburg in July, 1863. A female Union flag bearer was also killed in the same battle during Pickett's Charge. Sergeant Frank Mayne was killed serving in the Western Theater, but the soldier was actually a woman named Francis Day.

The Spanish American War: Twenty two women, all nurses, died in the service of their country. Of the 22, one death was undiagnosed, one died of Malaria, and twenty died of Typhoid Fever. Among the deceased were two African-Americans and five nuns. Nurse Clara Maass survived the war then volunteered to participate in an experimental treatment series for Typhoid Fever. The experiment killed her.

World War One: Nurses bore the brunt of fatalities but new roles began taking their toll among telephone operators, dieticians, Salvation Army women, Red Cross workers, YMCA volunteers, and military intelligence. Be it artillery shells, air raids, or natural deaths, 111 Army nurses died overseas, 186 perished stateside, over 20 US Navy Yeomen (females) died plus 27 women in the Navy Nurse Corps. The final tally was most likely in the hundreds.

World War Two: Army nurse Aleda Lutz was the first US military woman to perish in a combat zone during WWII when her hospital plane went down. She was on her 196th rescue mission. Six Army nurses lost their lives on Anzio Beach, four nurses who survived Anzio were awarded Silver Stars for courage under fire. Six nurses died and four were wounded when a Japanese Kamikaze aircraft struck their hospital ship USS *Comfort* in the South Pacific.

Four days after D-Day, Army nurse Lt. Francis Slanger and three other nurses were hit by shrapnel during a German artillery barrage. Slanger died from her injuries five months later in Boston. Over 400 military women lost their lives by the end of WWII. Treated shabbily by history, the WASPs (Women Airforce Service Pilots) lost 38 proficient female aviators transporting military aircraft.

The Korean War: From Ensigns to a Major, 15 nurses lost their lives in Korea. Non-hostile deaths claimed four more nurses.

Vietnam: *To be covered in my closing statements.*

Desert Storm (The Gulf War): Major Marie Rossi was flying a Chinook Cargo Chopper in bad weather when it hit an unlit tower. She was 32. Thirteen Army female soldiers died during Desert Storm and one Navy AG1. Stateside, Air National Guard Pilot Carol McKinney was lost.

Even during peacetime, America's lady warriors have made the supreme sacrifice. The first lady pilot in Navy history, Lt Cmdr. Barbara Rainey, was lost in an aircraft training accident in 1982. Lt. Colleen Cain, the first female HH-52A pilot in the Coast Guard, lost her life the same year when her chopper crashed into the side of a mountain. April 14, 1994: Lt. Laura Piper, an Air Force Academy graduate, was among the 26 people killed when Air Force fighter jets shot down two Army helicopters over Iraq. Lt. Kara Hultgreen, the first woman to qualify in Navy combat-ready F-14 Tomcats, perished in a freak crash while on final approach to the USS *Abraham Lincoln* on Oct 25, 1994. An engine malfunction caused the left engine to stall. Captain Amy Svoboda lost her life in the crash of an A-10 Thunderbolt. A Black Hawk helicopter crash in 1997 killed Spec Angela Niedermayer. AF Senior Master Sgt Sherry Olds lost her life in the 1998 bombing of the US embassy in East Africa. Army pilot Captain Jennifer Odem died when her reconnaissance aircraft hit the side of a mountain in southern Colombia in the war against narco-guerrillas.

Seven military women lost their lives in the Pentagon attack on 9/11, and as of this writing, the War on Terror has claimed the lives of over 150 females serving in uniform.

From the day we declared our independence to the rugged mountains of Afghanistan, women have served with honor and distinction. They are the mothers, daughters, sisters, nieces, girlfriends, fiancés, or just the girl next door who truly understand the cost of freedom. Pray for the ladies, as well as their brothers.

Women Of War And Words

The lieutenant was furious. In the midst of fighting on Iwo Jima, he was forced to discipline an aggressive photojournalist who had just snapped a series of pictures from atop an exposed ridge. He hollered, "That was the most damnable thing I ever saw anybody do in my life! Don't you realize that all the artillery and half the snipers on both sides of this damn war had ten full minutes to make up their mind about you?"

The 26 year old spitfire of a war correspondent was Georgette 'Dickey' Chappelle. Her actual assignment during the battle for Iwo Jima was to cover the activities of nurses onboard the hospital ship, USS *Samaritan*. Although repeatedly told not to leave the ship, Chappelle conned a press officer into believing that her story could best be photographed and reported from a field hospital behind the frontlines. Yet, once ashore, Chappelle headed straight for the combat zones.

She was not impressed with the barren landscape but decided to take photos of each section of battle surrounding the general area. Buzzing wasps were an aggravation that she kept swatting. Later, in her tent, Chappelle complained to her roommate about having to continually swat at wasps while taking photos. Her roommate laughed. "Iwo Jima is a volcanic island," she said. "There are no insects here. You were swatting at sniper bullets."

A feminist before feminism gained recognition, Chappelle's intelligence gained her admittance into the Massachusetts Institute of Technology (MIT) at the tender age of 16. An engineering student, her passion for journalism and photography won the day. She dropped out of MIT and spent the next three decades as a war correspondent. Interviewed on radio by a young upstart named Mike Wallace, Chappelle was asked if a 'woman's place' or a 'woman's job' was jumping out of airplanes, being at the front, and going on patrol with Marines.

The reply defined her determination: "It is not a woman's place," she said. "There's no question about that. There is only one other species on earth for whom a war zone is no place, and that's men. But as long as men continue to fight wars, I believe observers of both sexes will be sent to see what happens." Her work as a photographer and journalist earned Chappelle numerous awards plus respect from American soldiers.

November 4, 1965, south of Chu Lai, Vietnam: Chappelle is on a search and destroy mission with a Marine platoon when a lieutenant in front of her tripped a booby trap. Shrapnel from the explosion severed her carotid artery. Another photographer on the mission, Henri Huet, took the now famous photo of Chappelle receiving the last rites as she slowly bled to death. Georgette 'Dickey' Chappelle became the first US female war correspondent killed in action and the first correspondent to lose their life in Vietnam.

Women of war and words have a long history of dedication in the midst of danger. Journalist and women's rights advocate Margaret Fuller was America's first female war correspondent. As a staff writer for Horace Greeley of the New York Tribune, Fuller became the most-read person in New England, male or female, and was the first woman granted use of the library at Harvard College. Assigned to Europe in 1846, she sent back stories of the revolution in Italy and of the French bombardment of Rome. On the voyage back to the States in 1850, Fuller perished in a shipwreck off Fire Island, New York. Her body was never recovered.

While covering the attacks by Pancho Villa on American soil, Peggy Hull met General John 'Blackjack' Pershing. When WWI started, the US War Department denied her request to cover the war. Her connections with General Pershing paid off: she was allowed to spend two months at an artillery training camp in France until male journalists complained that she was not credentialed by the War Department. She was sent home. Another General she met in France pulled proper strings for Peggy and she became the first woman to be accredited by the War Department.

The War Department sent her to Siberia. Undeterred, Peggy reported on the Russian Revolution and the resulting Civil War. Years later, she was assigned to China to report on the invasion by Japan.

WWII presented the required catalyst for female war correspondents. Of 1,600 accredited journalists, 127 were women. Female journalists still tussled with skeptical military brass plus had to gather information without getting killed.

Helen Kirkpatrick, a graduate of Smith College and holder of a degree in International Law from the University of Geneva, worked as a freelance reporter before the war. Joining the staff of the Chicago Daily News in 1939, she reported from London during 'The Blitz' then accompanied the US Army to Algeria and the Mediterranean. She was with American forces during the Normandy Invasion in 1944 and was later attached to the Free French Forces, the first war correspondent to do so. In August of 1944, Kirkpatrick rode on top a tank of General Leclerc's 2nd Armored Division as they entered Paris. Her last assignment was Berchtesgaden, Hitler's mountain retreat in Bavaria, where she stole a frying pan from the kitchen.

Margaret Bourke-White, a renowned photographer, traveled for Life Magazine to the Soviet Union just as Germany broke their notorious non-aggression pact with the Communist country. She was the only foreign photographer in Moscow. She took refuge in the US Embassy and photographed the German siege of the city. Later, Bourke-White worked in the combat zones of Italy and Germany, and was under fire on several occasions.

Margaret Bourke-White

Many regarded Bourke-White as manipulative and uncaring. General Eisenhower disliked her. She traveled with General George Patton in the spring of 1945 to cover the collapse of Germany and took graphic photos of the Buchenwald concentration camp. Of the graphic photos, she stated, "Using a camera was almost a relief. It interposed a slight barrier between myself and the horror in front of me."

Martha Ellis Gellhorn, American travel writer, novelist, and journalist, is considered one of the greatest war correspondents of the 20th century. The third wife of novelist Ernest Hemingway and well-educated, Martha Gellhorn covered the Spanish Civil War and later reported on the rise of Adolph Hitler in Germany. She sent reports from Finland, Burma, Hong Kong, Singapore, and England. During the Normandy

Invasion, Gellhorn hid in a hospital ship bathroom then impersonated a stretcher bearer so she could hit the invasion beaches with American soldiers. She was the only woman to land in Normandy on D-Day, June 6, 1944.

Lee Miller's tragic early life took a turn for the better when the then-19 year old New York art student was saved from stepping into oncoming traffic by Conde Nast, the founder of Vogue. He recognized her beauty, launched her as Vogue cover girl in 1927, and she became a top model in New York. Bored with the modeling gig, Miller traveled to Paris, took up photography and befriended artists like Picasso and Max Ernst. She even appeared in a film. Her life was that of a bohemian, a free-spirited and free-thinking nonconformist; in today's jargon, a party animal.

When WWII broke out, Miller applied her photographic proficiencies to document the London Blitz. When America entered the war, her talent gained this free-spirited lady a new job as a war correspondent. Miller traveled with the 83rd Infantry Division from Normandy through Paris and into Germany. As one man said, "The GIs like her. They saw her as a good buddy. She could swear as well as they could, and put up with being under fire."

Lee Miller in Hitler's bathtub

On April 29, 1945, Miller walked through the gates of Dachau with the American forces. She was stunned by the sight, but took sickening and stark photos so future generations would 'never forget' the inhumanity to man. Later, Miller was with the GIs who discovered Hitler's apartment in Munich. The bohemian war correspondent couldn't resist the temptation: Miller had herself photographed naked in Hitler's bath.

Male war correspondents, from the superb reporting skills of Ernie Pyle of WWII celebrity to the hands-on reportage and hand-to-hand combat experiences of Joe Galloway in Vietnam, have been immortalized by the history of war. The ladies, too, have done their part to report the news from the battlefields. The male approach is hard-hitting facts, whereas the ladies pen with a touch of compassion rarely reported from the war zones. The ugliness of war requires both perspectives.

My Personal Tribute

Rest In Peace, My Sisters

War is not an attractive enterprise. It is brutal, indifferent, violent, the ultimate man-made killing machine. I experienced my war in Vietnam, along with 2.7 million other veterans of that conflict. And among those boots on the ground were women, just as dedicated and courageous as their male counterparts. A total of 67 American women lost their lives while serving in Southeast Asia; 59 civilians and eight military. The eight who perished in uniform will be personalized, yet the 59 civilians who died in that conflict, missionaries, Red Cross workers, CIA operatives, even a five month old baby girl, will be mentioned first, briefly.

Two died in jeep accidents: Hannah E. Crews and Rosalyn Muskat.

Two were murdered by U.S. soldiers: Virginia E. Kirsch and Marilyn L. Allan.

Four died of natural causes or unfortunate accidents: CIA employee Betty Gebhardt, Lucinda J. Richter, Regina "Reggie" William, and Dr. Breen Ratterman.

Catholic Relief Services worker, Gloria Redlin, was shot in Pleiku, 1969.

Army Special Services employee, Dorothy Phillips, died in a plane crash at Qui Nhon, 1967.

CIA operative, Barbara Robbins, died outside the American Embassy in Saigon on March 30, 1965, when a car bomb exploded.

Two female journalists were killed: Georgette "Dickey" Chappelle by a land mine while on a Marine patrol, and Phillipa Schuyler was killed in a firefight near Da Nang.

Janie A. Makil, the five month old daughter of missionary, Gasper Makil, was killed along with her father during an ambush at Dalat on March 4, 1963. They are buried together in the Philippines.

Evelyn Anderson and Beatrice Kosin were captured and burned to death in Kengkok, Laos in 1972. Their remains were recovered and returned to the U.S.

Missionary Eleanor Ardel Vietti was taken from the leprosarium in Ban Me Thuot on May 30, 1962. She is still listed as a POW.

A raid on the same leprosarium during the Tet Offensive in 1968 took the lives of four missionaries: Carolyn Griswald, Ruth Thompson, and Ruth Wilting. The fourth missionary, Betty Ann Olsen, was captured during the Tet Offensive raid. She died that same year in 1968 and was buried by a fellow POW, Michael Benge, the whereabouts unknown, along the Ho Chi Minh Trail in Laos. Her remains have never been recovered.

With communist forces making a final push to take Saigon in the spring of 1975, President Gerald Ford ordered the evacuation of Saigon orphans on a series of 30 planned flights. Between April 3 -26, 1975 approximately 3,300 infants and children were evacuated and eventually adopted by American and Allied families. Yet the first mission ended in tragedy.

A C-5A Galaxy lifted off the runway at Tan Son Nhut Airport a little after 4:00pm on April 4, 1975. Twelve minutes into the flight, the locks on the rear loading ramp failed. The ramp opened and separated, severing the rudder and elevators. The pilot and copilot wrestled the controls but to no avail, other than going to full power to keep the nose up. The massive cargo plane touched down in a rice paddy and skidded for a quarter of a mile, went airborne again for a half mile, then hit a dike and broke into four parts. There were survivors, but 138 people lost their lives, including 78 children. Of the American women aboard, including a teacher, a child, and various government workers, 38 were killed in the crash.

Barbara Adams • Clara Bayot • Nova Bell
Arleta Bertwell • Helen Blackburn • Ann Bottorff
Celeste Brown • Vivienne Clark • Juanita Creel
Mary Ann Crouch • Dorothy Curtis • Twila Donelson
Helen Drye • Theresa Drye • Mary Lyn Eichen
Elizabeth Fugino • Ruthanne Gasper • Beverly Herbert
Penelope Hindman • Vera Hollibaugh • Dorothy Howard
Barbara Kauvulia • Barbara Maier • Rebecca Martin
Sara Martini • Martha Middlebrook • Katherine Moore
Marta Moschkin • Marion Polgrean • June Poulton
JoanPray • Sayonna Randall • Anne Reynolds
Marjorie Snow • Laurie Stark • Barbara Stout
Doris Jean Watkins • Sharon Wesley

"There is in every true woman's heart a spark of heavenly fire, which lies dormant in the broad daylight of prosperity, but which kindles up and beams and blazes in the dark hour of adversity."
— Washington Irving

The Eight Female Warriors Who Gave Their All in Vietnam

Second Lieutenant Elizabeth Ann Jones was born and raised in Allendale, South Carolina. Carol Ann Elizabeth Drazba was born on December 11, 1943 in my father's hometown of Dunmore, Pennsylvania. Their duty assignment was in Saigon at the 3rd Field Hospital, 68th Medical Group. On February 18, 1966, they boarded a UH-1B Huey chopper of the 197th Assault Helicopter Company, 145th Combat Aviation Battalion for a flight to Da Lat. Over a river near Bien Hoa, the chopper struck a high-tension transmission and crashed. All seven persons aboard the Huey lost their lives, including Second Lieutenants Jones and Drazba. Both young ladies were 22 years old.

Lieutenant Colonel Annie Ruth Graham served her country for 26 years. Born in Efland, North Carolina on November 7, 1916, Lt. Col. Graham served in WWII, the Korean War, and Vietnam. Graham was serving as the Chief Nurse at the 91st Evacuation Hospital in Tuy Hoa, Vietnam when she suffered a massive stroke on August 14, 1968. Flown to Japan, she died four days later. Lt. Col. Graham was 52 years old.

Writing to her parents while stationed at the 312th Evacuation

Hospital in Chu Lai, First Lieutenant Sharon Ann Lane described the heat, the soldiers under her care, and a movie she missed the night before. She stated that things, "…were still very quiet around here, we haven't gotten mortared in a couple weeks now." Four days later, on June 8, 1969, the Viet Cong fired a barrage of 122mm into Chu Lai, many of the projectiles hitting the 312th Evacuation Hospital. One rocket hit between Wards 4A and 4B, wounding 27 and killing two. One of those killed was 1st Lt. Lane, who died instantly from shrapnel wounds to her chest. In one month, she would have been 26 years old.

Captain Eleanor Grace Alexander was stationed at the 85th Evacuation Hospital and First Lieutenant Hedwig Diane Orlowski at the 67th in Qui Nhon. They were temporarily pulling extra duty at the hospital in Pleiku due to heavy casualties in that area. On the return flight to Qui Nhon on November 30, 1967, the C-7B Caribou's pilot was advised the airfield at Qui Nhon was socked-in due to low cloud cover, rain, and low visibility. Diverted to Nha Trang, the C-7B Caribou crashed into a mountainside five miles from Qui Nhon. All 26 people aboard were killed, four aircrew and 22 passengers, included three male medical personnel and Captain Alexander, age 27, and First Lieutenant Orlowski, age 23.

Second Lieutenant Pamela Dorothy Donavan was assigned to the 85th Evacution Hospital in Qui Nhon. Born and raised in Ireland, the family moved to America when Pamela was a teenager. She had attended schools in Ireland, England, Canada, and eventually graduated from St. Elizabeth's Hospital School of Nursing in Boston as a registered nurse in 1965. The legal process for her to become a U.S. citizen was accelerated when she volunteered to serve as a nurse in Vietnam. She wrote to her parents on several occasions about 'the bravery of the boys on the front' and stated, 'their morale is good.' Four months into her assignment, 2nd Lt. Donavan contacted an unusual strain of Southeast Asian pneumonia and died on July 8, 1968.

The Last Lady Down

Captain Mary Therese Klinker was born in Lafayette, Indiana on October 3, 1947. In May of 1968 she graduated as a registered nurse from the St. Elizabeth's School of Nursing in Lafayette where she worked for about two years. She joined the USAF on January 9, 1970 as a Second Lieutenant, qualified as a flight nurse, and was promoted to Captain. Assigned to Clark Air Base in the Philippines, Captain Klinker was on the fateful first flight of Operation Babylift on April 4, 1975. As the C-5A Galaxy took off from Tan Son Nhut with orphans, civilian volunteers, and crewmembers, a rear door malfunction brought the massive plane down. Captain Mary Therese Klinker did not survive the crash. She was 27 years old, and the last American female warrior to die in the Vietnam War.

Closing Remarks

'Your mother wears combat boots!' Back in my early years those were fighting words, an insult of sorts, to provoke an adversary into a round of fisticuffs. Not today. Mothers do wear combat boots, and proudly, plus most of them can kick your supercilious civilian ass. America doesn't employ nor deploy girl soldiers; America just happens to have soldiers who are female. Lady warriors, past and present, were and are fashioned from the vital ingredients called mettle, sacrifice, resilience, responsibility, backbone, and aptitude. To hell with the sugar and spice.

Most ladies carry a purse; a select few tote 65 lb. rucksacks and an M-16. While other women shop together, warrior women clean their rifles with comrades. Women strut their stuff in high heels; others hit the ground with combat boots. Women paint on makeup to look pretty; some women paint on camouflage to stay alive. A spouse, girlfriend, daughter, can kiss the male she loves on a daily basis; warrior women kiss their males goodbye for a year.

The catchphrase *'all men are created equal'* is noted as the 'immortal declaration' in the Declaration of Independence from Great Britain and the 'single most important phrase' of the American Revolution with the greatest 'continuing importance' in meaning. In today's society, 'all women are created equal', but the best become soldiers.

About the Author

Pete is a graduate of Memphis State University with a BA Degree in Political Science and Public Administration with minors in Native American History and American Military History.

He served with Air Force Intelligence, including 2½ years in Vietnam.

Pete's full-page award-winning narrative *"A Veteran's Story"* is featured in several Georgia newspapers. He gives lectures and works as a consultant for TV, radio, and patriotic events.

His first book '*VETERANS: Stories From America's Best*' was published in April, 2018 featuring several of the 400+ veterans he has interviewed of all ranks, branches, and conflicts. '*FIGHTS LIKE A GIRL*' tells the stories of a variety of female warriors past and present, including a selection of his favorite interviews.

Pete has appeared on TV and radio, is an active keynote speaker, and serves as Commander of the prestigious Atlanta WWII Round Table.

He is a member of the North Georgia Veterans, Atlanta Vietnam Veterans Business Association, Military Order of World Wars, Churchill Society, VFW and American Legion, and other military-oriented organizations.

Contact Pete or send him your comments at: veteransarticle.com

CPSIA information can be obtained
at www.ICGtesting.com
Printed in the USA
FSHW011642130321
79421FS